Basic
HOMEBREWING

All the Skills and Tools You Need to Get Started

Stacy Tibbetts, editor

Jim Parker,
brewing consultant

photography by
James Collins

STACKPOLE
BOOKS

Published by
STACKPOLE BOOKS
5067 Ritter Road
Mechanicsburg, PA 17055
www.stackpolebooks.com

Printed in China

10 9 8 7 6 5 4 3 2 1

First edition

Cover design by Tracy Patterson
Photographs by James Collins
Illustrations by Caroline A. Stover

Library of Congress Cataloging-in-Publication Data

Basic homebrewing : all the skills and tools you need to get
started/ Stacy Tibbetts, editor ; Jim Parker, brewing consult-
ant ; photographs by James Collins.— 1st ed.
     p. cm.
   Includes bibliographical references and index.
   ISBN-13: 978-0-8117-3259-8
   ISBN-10: 0-8117-3259-2
   1. Brewing—Amateurs' manuals. I. Tibbetts, Stacy. II.
Parker, Jim, 1960–

TP570.B187   2005
641.8'73—dc22

2005016904

Contents

Acknowledgments

This book would not have been possible without the help of my good friend and active brewer Blair Malcom, whose love for the craft of brewing is strong, and whose patience for demonstrating the various processes knew no limits during our photo shoots. Prosit!

Here's a raised glass also to Jim Parker, whose guidance and expertise carried us through, and who provided first-rate recipes and sound advice on the best practices to illustrate for beginners.

It is always a pleasure to work with friend and photographer James Collins, who not only likes a good Irish stout, but whose professionalism, creativity, eye for detail, and high standards I first came to know and respect through his ongoing work for *Research Penn State* magazine. Cheers, James!

And for their help, special toasts also go out to Rich Pischke; Darrell Furfaro of Nittany Valley Feed and Hardware; Dave Staub of Zeno's in State College, PA; Mark Allison, Judith Schnell, Chris Chappell, and others at Stackpole Books; Jon Rounds; Diana, Lydia, and Wilson Malcom; Karen and Les Tibbetts; and Gretl and Dan Collins.

—Stacy Tibbetts

Introduction

Welcome to *Basic Homebrewing,* a guide to help you brew your first batches of beer. Everything you'll need to learn the craft is here:

- Detailed descriptions and photographs of the equipment you'll need.
- Information about the ingredients that go into beer—malted barley, hops, water, yeast, and other adjuncts.
- Step-by-step instructions for brewing seven different beer styles, each step accompanied by clear photographs that show you how to brew.
- An introduction to some advanced brewing techniques and equipment.
- A list of publications and organizations where you can find supplies and information.

You'll learn how to brew several classic beers—an amber ale, a pale ale, a porter, a stout, and a lager—as well as two more unusual beers: a barley wine and a witbier, or white beer. One chapter is devoted to each beer style, and each chapter includes the following:

- A clear list and photograph of the necessary ingredients.
- The history, unique characteristics, and commercially available examples of the style.
- A graphic that shows you the timing for adding the ingredients.
- Clear, illustrated, step-by-step instructions for brewing the beer.

In addition, each successive chapter introduces new techniques into the brewing process, so you'll develop your skills and expertise as you try new styles.

Parker's Amber Ale, a very basic brew, is the first recipe. This introduces you to culturing yeast, boiling and adding the ingredients, adding the yeast (called pitching) and beginning the fermentation, monitoring the fermentation, and bottling the brew. The importance of cleanliness and sanitation is emphasized throughout the book.

Brewing our Paradise Pale Ale will introduce you to the techniques of wort chilling and dry hopping. The Parliamentary Porter recipe teaches you how to handle roasted barley grains and add them to your beer for flavor and color. The Old Bald Fart Barley Wine chapter sums up the techniques introduced in the first three recipes, as it requires a yeast starter culture, added grains, and dry hopping.

The Moo-Juice Milk Stout recipe introduces the addition of adjunct ingredients (in this case, lactose), as well as kegging and force-carbonating your beer in the keg, using carbon dioxide. The Old Country Lager chapter explains the lagering process for producing clean, crisp, traditional German brews. Finally, the Wedding Wit beer, a more complex recipe, uses spices and a mini-mash before the boil to steep and extract flavor from added grains.

At the heart of brewing is the process of fermentation, which involves the action of yeast on sugars to produce alcohol and carbon dioxide. Learning how to control this process to produce your own tasty creations will appeal to those interested in cooking, chemistry, or just high-quality beer and the pleasure of creating and sharing it with friends and family. Best of luck to you as you begin your adventure into *Basic Homebrewing.*

Equipment and Ingredients

Most of the basic tools you'll need to start brewing are available in beginners' kits. These usually include plastic or glass fermentation containers, a bottle capper, airlocks, corks, hoses, and possibly a hydrometer or thermometer. Available at reputable suppliers for around $50 or $60, these kits can be a good way for the absolute beginner to get started, since they include nearly everything you'll need to make your first batch. Most kits don't include a boiling kettle, though, so you'll have to supply that on your own. It's a good idea to check with a store clerk to make sure you have everything you need.

For more adventuresome brewers, or those who already own a bit of equipment, the à la carte method of buying gear is the way to go. Sometimes you can pull together the necessary individual pieces of equipment for a price that is quite comparable to that of a kit—and you might also enjoy scrounging at your local hardware or restaurant supply store for an unusual or high-quality bit of gear.

The kit on the previous page includes a 5-gallon glass carboy with a carrying handle, rubber stopper, and airlock; a plastic primary fermenter bucket; a glass Erlenmeyer flask with stopper and airlock; a kitchen strainer, boiling kettle, and stainless-steel spoon; a bottle capper, filler, brush, and caps; a hydrometer and a dairy thermometer; a racking cane and siphon hose for transferring beer between containers; and mesh sacks for steeping grains before the boil.

Familiarity with the basic ingredients that go into beer is also essential for a first-timer. Common varieties of malted barley, which provides body and the basic character of your beer, include liquid malt extract, powdered dried malt extract, and malted and roasted barley grains. Hops, a plant whose oily, aromatic flowers provide the beer's bitterness, smell, and bite, comes in both plug and pellet form. (It is also sold in a loose-leaf form, not shown in the photograph.) Other ingredients include yeast for fermentation and priming sugar for in-the-bottle carbonation.

This chapter illustrates and further describes the equipment and ingredients you'll need to start brewing. Essential tools are given first, followed by ingredients, and then optional and additional tools that might be helpful as you gain experience. Each item is accompanied by a description of what it does and how it is used.

Essential Tools

KETTLE

Although the choice of a brewing kettle is often determined by what's available in your home kitchen, you should not brew with anything smaller than a 4-gallon kettle. This will enable you to comfortably boil 3 gallons of wort (the term for beer in the process of being brewed) then add 2 gallons of cooling water in the fermentation container to make a standard 5-gallon batch of beer. Larger kettles that enable you to boil an entire 5 gallons are preferable but not as readily available. Stainless steel is recommended.

SPOON

The spoon also should be stainless steel to avoid contaminating your beer with bacteria or other microorganisms that can live on the surface of plastic or wooden utensils. It should be large enough to allow you to easily stir a full brewing kettle.

POTS AND PANS

Additional smaller pots and pans are essential for various procedures, including heating water to rinse grains and boiling small amounts of extract for yeast starter cultures. A large (8-quart) pot is needed for the mashing process in Chapter 8, when making the Wedding Wit. A heavy-bottomed pot works best for maintaining a steady temperature in the mash.

THERMOMETER

A thermometer is essential for determining the temperature of your heated wort as you add ingredients. It also helps you determine when the wort has cooled enough to add, or pitch, the yeast. A floating dairy thermometer (top left) is easy to use and keep clean, and has a wide temperature range. A kitchen dial thermometer (top right) can be clipped to the side of a kettle easily but may not indicate lower temperatures needed for yeast pitching. An inexpensive strip thermometer (bottom) can be stuck to the side of a fermentation container to monitor temperatures.

HYDROMETER

A hydrometer measures the specific gravity, or density, of a liquid. By taking hydrometer readings of your beer before and after fermentation, you can determine the amount of alcohol it contains. Instructions for using a hydrometer are given in Chapter 2.

BASTER

Use a kitchen baster to pull samples of hot liquid from your boiling kettle, or fermenting wort from your fermenter, and place them in the hydrometer tube.

AIRLOCKS

Airlocks are used to prevent air from entering the fermentation containers while allowing carbon dioxide gas to bubble out. Both the bubble lock (left) and econo-lock (right) are filled halfway with water when in use.

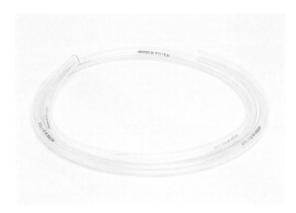

TUBING

A section of clear rubber tubing is essential for siphoning your beer between fermenters or into bottles. Four feet should be plenty, and tubing with a $3/8$-inch inside diameter will fit well over hard plastic racking canes or bottle fillers. Tubing is often available in hardware stores—make sure it is food-grade quality before you buy it.

STOPPERS

Drilled rubber stoppers are used to attach airlocks to fermenters.

FERMENTATION CONTAINERS

For most homebrewed beer, fermentation occurs at room temperature. Because of the lack of refrigeration, this process must take place in a sanitized, closed container to prevent contamination of the wort with microorganisms. The most available and commonly used container is the plastic food-grade bucket (left). It should be unscratched and spotless inside, and you should sanitize it before use. A specially designed one with gradations and a draincock (center) is useful for transferring your beer to bottles or a secondary fermenter, should you use one.

Because it can be kept very clean, a 5-gallon glass carboy (shown at right with a detachable carrying handle) is the most preferable fermentation vessel. It can be used as the primary fermenter in a one-step fermentation or the secondary vessel in a two-step fermentation.

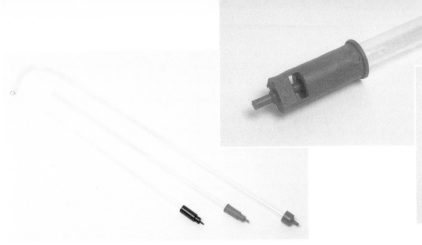

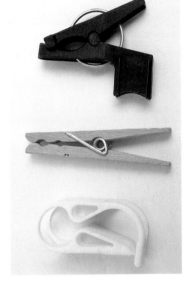

BOTTLE FILLERS AND RACKING CANE

In the top left photo, two bottle fillers lie to the left of a curved racking cane. The bottle fillers have a spring-loaded tip (top center), which is pressed against the bottom of the bottle to allow careful regulation of the beer flow. The racking cane has a fixed extension tip (top right), which prevents the siphoning off of yeast sediment from the bottom of the fermenter.

CLIPS

Racking canes and siphon hoses can be attached to the sides of containers with various types of clips.

STRAINER

A large (6 to 8 inches in diameter) kitchen strainer is used to clear the wort as you pour it into the fermenter, particularly if you've used loose hops. As with all other utensils you'll use when brewing, stainless steel is best, and the strainer should be sanitized before use.

CHEESECLOTH AND BUNGEE CORDS

You can also use cheesecloth for straining, fastening it to the top of a plastic fermenter with the cords.

MESH BAGS

Reusable plastic mesh bags, which come in various sizes, are handy for steeping grains before you boil the wort.

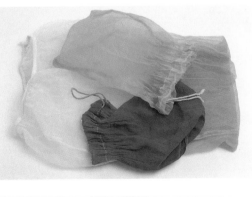

CHEESECLOTH BAGS

Smaller disposable cheesecloth bags, sometimes called hops sacks, can be used for adding hops. All bags can be loosely tied, twist-tied shut, or clipped to the side of the kettle.

5

CULTURING CONTAINERS

Generally speaking, the more live yeast that can be added to a batch of wort, the faster the fermentation will begin. You can add commonly available liquid yeast directly from the manufacturer's pouch or vial, or culture it in advance by placing it in a weak wort solution. Use an Erlenmeyer flask (far left) or a glass milk bottle from your local dairy (near left) to culture yeast, along with a small funnel to fill it. More information about yeast and yeast culturing is provided in Chapter 2.

WHISK

A whisk can be used to aerate the wort before the yeast is pitched. The more oxygen that is dissolved in the wort, the faster the yeast will begin to reproduce and ferment the beer, and the better it will taste. Advanced homebrewers sometimes buy aquarium aeration pumps and connect them to submersible aeration stones to produce tiny, soluble bubbles in the wort. Whisking or even shaking the wort before pitching is a more affordable way to go.

RUBBING ALCOHOL

Use rubbing alcohol to sterilize both the yeast packet and the scissors needed to open it. Make every effort to maintain cleanliness and prevent bacterial contamination of the fermenting wort.

SCISSORS

Used to open the yeast packet.

STANDARD BOTTLES

Most beginning homebrewers bottle their beer. This affordable option allows you to collect and reuse your own bottles, which come in various sizes and shapes. A 5-gallon batch of beer will fill fifty-three 12-ounce bottles or forty 16-ounce bottles. Avoid collecting twist-off bottles, which can't be easily recapped.

SWING-TOP BOTTLES

Another attractive option is the swing-top bottle. On the left is a large growler, sometimes available from microbreweries, which typically holds 2 liters of beer. On the right is a smaller 16-ounce version. When sterilizing a bottle with a swing-top cap, pry off the ceramic cap and the metal hooks that hold it, and drop the entire apparatus in a sanitizing solution.

BOTTLE CAPS

Uncrimped bottle caps are available in bulk from most brewing-supply stores. Submerge them in a sterilizing solution before use.

BOTTLE-CLEANING BRUSH

A good bottle-cleaning brush is a mandatory purchase. A standard foot-long brush with a wire handle and circular bristles (center) for scouring the debris from used bottles is the most useful. A larger brush with a bent head (top) is good for cleaning glass carboys, and a smaller two-headed brush (bottom) works well for cleaning plastic fermenter drains, funnels, stoppers, and other small pieces of equipment.

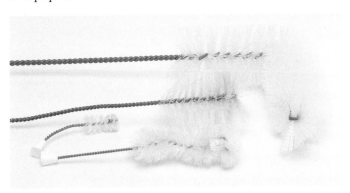

BOTTLE CAPPER

A bottle capper is an essential piece of equipment if you plan to bottle your brew. A bench-top capper (with the long handle) can be fastened to a solid surface. A wing-type capper (below) is simply placed on top of the bottle that is being capped.

COMMERCIAL CLEANERS

Cleaning and sanitizing *all* of the equipment that comes into contact with the wort, especially after it is cooled, is essential to successful brewing. More information about cleaning and sanitizing is given in Chapter 2. Household bleach will work as a cleaner and sanitizer, but it leaves a residue that must be rinsed off before any equipment can be used. Other commercial cleaners and sanitizers include professional iodine-based sanitizers such as Iodophor liquid; B-Brite (a cleaner only, not a sanitizer); and the recommended One-Step powder, which does not require a rinse if used in the proper amount. Professional acid-based sanitizers are often used by commercial breweries and may be useful as you expand your setup.

Ingredients

The basic ingredients that are used to brew beer are water, malted barley, hops, and yeast. Germany even has a national brewing standard, called the Reinheitsgebot ("purity law"), which specifies that most of its beers must use only these four ingredients. Sometimes breweries use other, less expensive grains such as corn and wheat in place of barley, typically producing much lighter-bodied beers. Other additives abound in large-scale, mass-market brewing, particularly in America.

Although much is made of the ingredients that go into beer, most of the differences among readily available beers result from varying the type or processing of the ingredients or the way they are added. Barley can be roasted lighter or darker; the type of hops can be more or less bitter; and a particular strain of yeast adds a distinct character and aroma.

For example, Chapter 3 of this book teaches dry hopping as a way of giving extra hops character to a pale ale. Chapters 4 and 5 teach you how to use specialty dark-roasted grains to brew a porter and a barley wine, both darker styles of beer. Chapter 7 introduces lager yeast and lagering to produce a specific lighter style of beer with a different type of fermentation.

Other specialty beers can be made by adding or substituting other ingredients, such as grains and fruit flavorings. Chapter 6 teaches you how to brew a milk stout, which uses lactose to create a fuller-bodied dark beer. The Wedding Wit recipe in Chapter 8 uses wheat and oats to create a characteristic cloudy wort and includes spices in the boil.

BARLEY GRAINS

Four degrees of roasted, malted barley grains are shown below. The malting process for barley involves partially germinating the grains, usually by soaking them in water, then drying them. This develops sugars and starches, which are useful in the brewing process.

The lightest grain is a two-row malt, which has relatively more starch and fewer sugars. This type of grain is used most often in beer as a base malt and requires a process called mashing—heating and soaking at a specified temperature—to convert the starches to sugars. This process is often used by advanced homebrewers and is briefly introduced in Chapters 8 and 9. Most beginning brewers, however, use a commercially available extract for a base malt; this is a processed version of malted barley in which the grains have been mashed and steeped—soaked in hot water before the boil—and the resulting liquid has been thickened into a syrup or dried into a powder.

The copper-colored grain is a good example of a crystal malt, one in which more of the starch has been converted to usable sugar. Some of the sugars in crystal malts become caramelized during the drying process. These malts are used most often in beer to add color and flavor to the base malt, and they can be simply steeped to wash out the sugars and flavors. This process is covered in Chapters 4 and 5. The varying degrees of darkness in crystal malts are described using the Lovibond scale. Most crystal malts fall into the 10°L to 120°L range.

The darker grains (a chocolate malt and a black malt) are roasted malts, which have been dried at higher temperatures or for longer periods of time than crystal malts. As a result, their sugars become charred instead of caramelized. Roasted malts are often cracked and steeped in hot water before the boil to produce specialty beers such as porters and stouts.

LIQUID MALT EXTRACT

Liquid malt extract forms the base malt for most beginning homebrews, and all of the recipes in this book use it as the first ingredient. It is made by mashing and steeping grains, then drying the resulting wort into a thick syrup.

Liquid malt extract is available in different degrees of darkness, from pale to amber to dark. Flavors and shadings vary among manufacturers. Some sell extract in cans (above right), as well as in bulk to distributors, which package it in plastic containers (above left and center). Purchasing a reputable brand such as Muntons, Alexander's, or Briess will ensure that you're getting a quality product, made with malted barley grains only.

DRIED MALT EXTRACT

Dried malt extract is made by concentrating liquid malt extract and spray-drying it into a powder. Like liquid malt extract, it is sold in different degrees of darkness. Good brands include Muntons and Fison's and Laaglander extracts, the latter distributed by LD Carlson.

Although entire batches of beer can be brewed with dried malt extract, it is more expensive than the liquid form. As a result, it is often added to the base liquid malt in a recipe to provide extra body or character. In this book, the pale ale, stout, lager, and witbier recipes call for DME. Having a bag on hand is useful for making yeast starter cultures as well. See Chapter 2 for more about this process.

HOPS

In a good beer, hops are the yin to malt's yang, the Felix Unger to malt's Oscar Madison, the perfect foil that adds bite and bitterness to malt's sweetness. Hops are the inflorescences, or flowers, of the hops vine. This plant can be grown anywhere, but commercial production is centered in Germany, southern England, southern Australia, and Washington State. Hops are most commonly sold in three forms: as whole cones or flowers (left); semicompressed plugs (center); and hard, compressed pellets (right). Although the different forms contribute slightly different levels of bitterness to a beer per ounce, they can be used interchangeably in most recipes.

The individual petals of the hops flowers are coated with an oily yellow resin called lupulin. This resin soaks off when the hops are boiled in the wort, providing a beer's distinct bitter character. Oxygen and heat can deteriorate the quality of fresh hops, making the lupulin oils rancid, so hops should be stored in the refrigerator.

Different hops varieties have very different degrees of bitterness. The percentage of alpha acid resins in the hops flower (beta acid resins are also present) is used as a measure of this characteristic. It is represented in alpha acid units (AAU), where 1 AAU equals 1 percent alpha acid in the flower. Certain hops are 6 percent AAU; others are 9 or even 10 percent. (See the table below.) Alpha acid resins are not readily soluble in water, so the hops must be boiled for 30 to 90 minutes to create optimum conditions for the alpha acids to dissolve and provide a beer's bitter character. Thus, bittering hops are the first hops to be added to the boil.

Finally, because it is a flower, hops also can add flavor and aroma (bouquet) to a beer, in addition to bitterness. Certain aromatic and volatile oils in the hops flower will dissolve very quickly in the wort and evaporate if they boil for too long. Therefore, additional hops are added later in the boil to create these qualities. Flavoring hops are added midboil, and finishing hops are typically added to a beer during the final few minutes of the boil to give it a distinct nose. Dry hopping (covered in Chapters 3 and 5) is the addition of dry hops to the fermenter before the beer is bottled, which imparts intense aroma and bouquet.

Common Hops Varieties

Hops name	Alpha acid content*	Common use and notes
Brewers Gold	8–9 AAU	Traditional ale hops; loses bitterness in storage
Bullion	8–9 AAU	Bittering hops; poor aroma
Cascade	5–6.5 AAU	Bittering and aroma hops; citrusy
Chinook	11–13 AAU	Very bitter; maintains bitterness well in storage
Fuggles	4–5.5 AAU	Traditional British ale bittering and aroma hops
Goldings	4.5–5.5 AAU	Traditional British ale bittering and aroma hops
Hallertauer	4.5–5.5 AAU	Traditional lager hops; spicy flavor and aroma
Kent Goldings	4.5–5.5 AAU	Traditional British ale bittering and aroma hops
Northern Brewer	7.5–9 AAU	Traditional European lager bittering hops
Perle	7–9 AAU	Similar to Northern Brewer
Saaz	4–6 AAU	Traditional pilsener lager hops; spicy flavor and good aroma
Tettnanger	4–6 AAU	Lager hops; American variety is floral; German is spicier
Willamette	5–6 AAU	Similar to Fuggles; excellent aroma, ale or lager hops

*For hops substitutions within a recipe, choose one with a similar alpha acid content and similar usage, such as bittering, flavor, or aroma.

YEAST

Yeast is an organism—technically a fungus—that lives on the beer wort while creating fermentation. It contributes as much to the final flavor of a beer as do the malt and hops. It is important to note that brewer's yeasts are different from ordinary bread yeasts. (More information on yeasts and fermentation is available in Chapter 2.) The two main varieties of beer yeast are ale yeast, which ferments best at 55 to 75°F (13 to 24°C), and lager yeast, which ferments at cooler temperatures (32 to 55°F, 0 to 13°C). Lagering—storing beers at cold temperatures after the process of fermentation—is discussed in Chapter 7. Hundreds of unique strains of ale and lager yeasts are commercially available.

Although dried brewer's yeasts (bottom left) are available, their use in basic homebrewing is not recommended for several reasons. First, they are often sold simply as undifferentiated brewer's yeast, which does not allow for the use of a yeast strain appropriate for the type of beer being brewed, such as an Irish ale yeast or a Bavarian lager yeast. Second, if you just sprinkled a small amount of dry yeast onto a wort, it would take a long time for the yeast to multiply to the level at which fermentation can begin. Underpitching, or using insufficient yeast, can give bacteria or microorganisms a chance to develop in the wort. The beer also may stop fermenting too soon, leaving it too sweet. If dried brewer's yeast is the only option, a starter culture (see Chapter 2) should be made.

The best yeast choice for homebrewers is a pitchable liquid variety (bottom right). These yeasts are contained in a small amount of starter culture, which allows them to feed and reproduce to a level that produces relatively rapid fermentation when they are added to the wort.

The gold-colored Wyeast smack pack has been the standard choice of homebrewers for several years. It contains a small internal packet of starter culture that is broken by smacking the outer package with the heel of the hand, mixing it with the yeast in the outer packet. This is done one to two days before brewing, depending on the freshness of the packet.

The yeast can then be added to the brew directly or increased further (for more rapid fermentation) by placing it into a second, homemade starter culture. Technically, a starter culture is necessary to produce the optimum amount of yeast for pitching into a 5-gallon batch of beer.

The vial of California Labs yeast shown below contains an amount of yeast similar to the gold Wyeast smack pack. The blue Activator smack pack to its right is the newest Wyeast product. It contains sufficient yeast and wort to produce a pitchable yeast culture for a 5-gallon batch of beer within hours of smacking the package, without making a starter culture.

All recipes in this book assume the use of liquid yeast, and they require readily available strains. Yeast should be purchased fresh from the manufacturer. Advanced brewers sometimes culture their own yeast, saving it from previous batches of beer.

PRIMING SUGAR

Priming sugar is typically corn sugar, which sometimes can be bought in a grocery store. This sugar is added in small quantities after the beer has been bottled to produce carbonation. It does this by providing additional food for the yeast, starting a second mini-fermentation in the bottle that creates carbon dioxide. If the beer is bottled, the gas dissolves in the liquid, producing fizziness.

SPECIALTY INGREDIENTS

Additional specialty ingredients can be added to produce unique beers. Oats can be steeped in hot water before the boil to create an oatmeal stout. Fruit extracts or even crushed fruit can be added to beer to produce exceptional flavors. Spices such as cloves are often added to holiday beers. Chapter 6 introduces the use of lactose powder to create a milk stout, and the Wedding Wit recipe in Chapter 8 uses flaked wheat and oats, as well as dried orange peel, coriander, and grains of paradise (see page 67).

Water Quality

Should you worry about your water quality for making beer? The short answer is probably not. Most reputable sources of drinking water will produce decent beers. Removing excess chlorine from some municipal water supplies is recommended, however. Do this by running it through a commercial charcoal filter (now common as a faucet attachment or in the top of a water pitcher) or boiling it before using.

Very soft water, which lacks mineral content, can be improved by adding a small amount of gypsum, usually 1 to 4 teaspoons for a 5-gallon batch. An excess of minerals, however, will ruin a beer, so check with your local water department, and add gypsum only if your water contains less than 50 parts per million (ppm) of calcium. If you are using malt extract, adding minerals will usually be unnecessary, since they were introduced into the extract when it was made from the original grains.

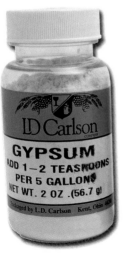

ADDITIVES

Other optional beer ingredients are additives that produce certain effects or refine the finished product. Gypsum (calcium sulfate) is sometimes added to water to produce calcium ions, which increase hardness and help clarify the beer during fermentation. It also adds a crispness to the character of hoppy beers such as pale ales and India pale ales.

Irish moss is a coagulant that uses a molecular electrostatic charge to attract precipitated proteins in the boiling wort and pull them out of solution; this also clarifies the beer. During the last ten to fifteen minutes of a boil, $1/4$ to $1/2$ teaspoon is added. Irish moss is listed in this book's recipes as an optional ingredient.

Optional Tools

The following tools and equipment are not essential for basic brewing. As you get comfortable with the process and begin to try more advanced techniques, however, you may find some of them useful.

BOTTLE WASHER
A high-speed water-jet bottle washer is extremely handy for cleaning and rinsing bottles. An angled tube screws onto a water faucet or hose. A pressure-sensitive release valve at the other end is activated when an empty bottle is pressed onto it. The hose-threaded adapter coupling can be attached to any kitchen sink faucet.

DRYING TREE
A plastic bottle-drying tree makes this process a lot neater.

GRAIN MILL
If you decide to move into all-grain brewing, you may want to buy a grain mill, which allows you to crack large quantities of grains for mashing. The model shown can be operated with the removable hand crank or an electric drill.

SCALE
A small kitchen scale can be handy for measuring small quantities of grains and hops. Get one that allows you to zero the gauge after you place an empty container on it.

MORTAR AND PESTLE
A mortar and pestle can be used to grind and crush small quantities of spices. A coffee bean grinder also does this well.

ROLLING PIN
Use a rolling pin to crack small quantities of specialty grains for steeping before the boil. This process is described in chapters 4 and 5.

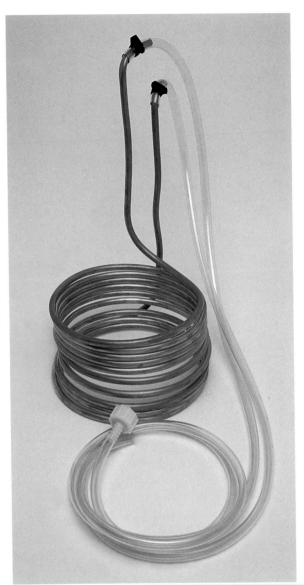

WORT CHILLERS

To improve the quality of basic homebrew, the single most important piece of additional equipment you can buy or make is a wort chiller.

The simplest type to use is the copper tubing immersion chiller at left. Twenty-five feet or more of coiled copper tubing is attached to a kitchen faucet with rubber hoses, and the coil is submerged in the hot wort. Rapid circulation of cold water through the tubing cools the wort quickly so that the yeast can be pitched. This improves the flavor of the beer and reduces the chances of contamination while cooling is taking place. More information about making and using wort chillers is available in Chapter 3.

The counterflow chiller on the bottom left is made from a length of copper tubing threaded through a garden hose, which is then coiled. The hot wort is siphoned through the copper tubing in one direction, while cold water is run through the hose in the opposite direction. This type of chiller is very effective but harder to keep clean than an immersion chiller.

A PVC tube chiller like the one on the bottom right can be made by coiling a copper tube inside a sealed length of PVC pipe. As with the counterflow chiller, the beer flows through the inner coil while cold water is flooded into the plastic pipe. This type of chiller can be mounted easily onto a permanent brewing setup and connected to a brewing kettle that has a drain fitting. This picture shows the two fittings for attaching the water and wort hoses to the chiller. Similar fittings are located on the other end of the tube.

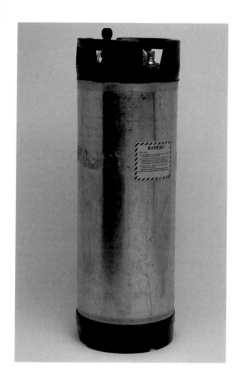

KEG

Doing away with bottles and the bottling process will be a welcome relief for many homebrewers. By far the most widely used kegging setup involves the 5-gallon soda keg, otherwise known as the Cornelius keg, or corny keg. This can be easily attached to a carbon dioxide tank for quicker carbonation and dispensing of your brew. More information about using kegs and carbon dioxide equipment can be found in Chapter 6.

CARBON DIOXIDE TANK

Shown on the near right is a typical set of carbon dioxide regulating gauges, attached to a small carbon dioxide tank. Use these to inject carbon dioxide into a keg of beer after you've brewed and to maintain low pressure on the keg while you're dispensing the beer. A more typical carbon dioxide tank is also shown on the far right.

CHEST FREEZER

A chest freezer like the one on the left or an old upright refrigerator makes a good keg fridge. You can regulate the temperature on a refrigerator or freezer with an external control unit such as the one shown inset, made by Johnson Controls. The sensor is placed in the refrigerator or freezer, and the desired temperature is set on the dial. The control regulates the electricity flow through the refrigerator's power cord. Advanced models have circuitry that protects against rapid on-off cycling of the refrigerator's compressor unit. These devices also can be used for lagering.

2

Basic Techniques
Parker's Amber Ale

This chapter illustrates and describes the steps in the process of brewing your first basic batch of beer, from starting the yeast culture to bottling. The process spans about two weeks, with an additional week or so required for your beer to carbonate in the bottles before you can drink it. Below is a timeline of a typical complete brewing process.

About Parker's Amber Ale
An ale is a beer that is made with a top-fermenting yeast, one that often temporarily gathers at the top of the container during fermentation before settling to the bottom. Ales are traditional British beer styles. They are fermented between 55 and 70°F (13 and 21°C) and are one of the easiest types of beer for a beginning home-

1–2 days	2–3 days	6–11 days	7–10 days
Yeast Culturing	Primary Fermentation	Secondary Fermentation	Bottle Conditioning and Carbonation

Starting the Yeast (optional)
About an hour

Brew Day
4–5 hours

Transfer to Secondary Fermenter (optional)
About an hour

Bottling
2–3 hours

Sampling
Many pleasant hours

Ingredients

- [ ] 6.5 pounds amber malt extract
- [ ] 0.5 ounce Northern Brewer hops, 60 minutes
- [ ] 0.5 ounce Willamette hops, 30 minutes
- [ ] 0.5 ounce Willamette hops, 10 minutes
- [ ] Wyeast 1056, American Ale yeast
- [ ] priming sugar for bottling

Optional

- [ ] dry malt extract for the yeast starter culture
- [ ] 0.5 teaspoon Irish moss (add during last 10 minutes of boil)

Ingredient Timing

:00 Boil begins
Add 0.5 ounce Northern Brewer hops

:30 Add 0.5 ounce Willamette hops

:50 Add another 0.5 ounce Willamette hops
Add 0.5 teaspoon Irish moss (optional)

:60 Remove from heat

Original Specific Gravity:	**1.046**
Final Specific Gravity:	**1.010**

Filled with mingled cream and amber,
I will drain that glass again.
Such hilarious visions clamber
Through the chamber of my brain—
Quaintest thoughts—queerest fancies
Come to life and fade away;
What care I how time advances?
I am drinking ale today.

—"Lines on Ale," Edgar Allan Poe

brewer to make. Some familiar ales include Sam Adams Boston Ale, Fat Tire Amber Ale, and Rogue American Amber.

Parker's Amber Ale is named after Jim Parker, editor of *Zymurgy* magazine, former director of the American Homebrewers Association, and a consultant on this book. It uses an amber, or slightly darker, extract to pro-vide a full, rich flavor. The classic style of British ale that it most closely resembles is an English bitter. British brewers might use Brewers Gold, Bullion, Kent Goldings, Fuggles, or Northern Brewer hops in a bitter. This recipe adds Willamette to the boil—a Fuggles hybrid grown in Oregon, Jim Parker's home state—to lend a uniquely American character.

A yeast starter culture is a very small batch of weak beer that serves as nutrient for the yeast, allowing it to multiply before you add it to your beer. Make the culture one or two days before your brewing day to allow time for the yeast to grow. Making a yeast starter culture is good practice for actual brewing, as it emphasizes the need for sanitation, and it creates your first fermentation—the process that is at the heart of brewing.

Equipment Needed

- [ ] Erlenmeyer flask or glass bottle
- [ ] airlock
- [ ] rubber stopper
- [ ] small pan
- [ ] measuring cup
- [ ] funnel
- [ ] dairy thermometer
- [ ] kitchen scissors
- [ ] rubbing alcohol

Ingredients Needed

- [ ] dried malt extract (DME)
- [ ] Wyeast packet (or other brewer's yeast)
- [ ] tap water

Adding the correct amount of yeast to your beer (around 200 billion cells for a typical 5-gallon batch) will help the fermentation begin quickly, creating better-tasting beer. Technically, a full-strength yeast starter culture should be one-tenth the size of the batch of beer. (For a 5-gallon batch, this would mean creating a $^1/_2$-gallon-size starter.) The Wyeast package instructions suggest a 1-pint starter culture to grow the original 40 to 60 billion cells provided in the package. Larger starter cultures may begin the fermentation more quickly but will take longer to create and may also change the flavor of your beer.

1. Sanitize the Erlenmeyer flask, dairy thermometer, cork, and airlock by soaking in a solution of water and household bleach. (A 1-gallon glass jug or glass milk bottle will also work, as long as the cork seals it tightly.) See the "Cleaning and Sanitizing" sidebar on pages 22–23 for more information.

2. Boil a pint of water and add $^1/_2$ cup of dried malt extract in a small (one-quart) pan.

3. Stir in the extract and boil for 10 minutes. This will make a weak wort, or beer solution, with a specific gravity of 1.02 to 1.04. (See page 29 for an explanation of specific gravity.)

4. Fill the flask with the wort.

About Yeast and Fermentation

Yeast is a single-cell living organism, technically a fungus. It reproduces rapidly, and when added to your beer, it goes through several phases and activities. During the height of an active fermentation, each milliliter of your beer may contain as many as 50 million yeast cells!

Yeasts perform respiration, the process of gaining energy; fermentation, expending energy by converting sugars to alcohol, carbon dioxide, and flavor; and sedimentation, collecting together and drifting to the bottom of the container when fermentation is complete.

When sugars are no longer available, the yeast cells go dormant but do not die. As a result, yeast from a completed fermentation can be saved and reused. Some avid microbrewers keep favorite cultures on hand, and others even retrieve jars of spent yeast from small commercial brewpubs. Doing this within a week of the completed fermentation provides the most viable yeast.

Yeasts need the proper temperature, pH, nutrients, and oxygen to produce an active fermentation. Most ale yeasts *(Saccharomyces cerevisiae)* work best at 60 to 75°F (16 to 24°C). Lager yeasts *(Saccharomyces uvarum)* work best at 35 to 50°F (2 to 10°C). Chilling yeasts slows them down and makes them go dormant. Warmer temperatures may make some yeasts work faster but also increases the risk of bacterial contamination. Temperatures above 120°F (49°C) will kill the yeasts. When transferring yeast to a new environment, such as from the refrigerator to a starting wort, gradually warm the yeasts to the new temperature rather than abruptly shocking them.

Yeasts work best at a slightly acidic pH (4.5 to 5.5). This type of environment occurs readily in beer wort and should not be a concern to the beginning brewer. Nutrients likewise are present in the malt extracts you'll be using. Oxygen, however, is an important requirement of yeast respiration, and the lack of oxygen can slow down initial yeast activity. Splash or whisk the wort in the fermenter *before* adding the yeast. Bubbling oxygen into the wort also helps.

During the first four to eight hours that the yeast is in your beer, it will multiply rapidly and undergo respiration. No alcohol is produced during this time period. Fermentation quickly follows, and the yeasts continue to reproduce during this time period. Finally, sedimentation and dormancy take place anywhere from three to seven days after the yeast has been added.

Yeasts may occasionally produce flavors that are fruity, butterscotchlike, cidery, grassy, or solventlike. Most of these are the result of chemicals produced during respiration: esters and diacetyl. These are not dangerous or poisonous, but they are usually undesirable if they are too pronounced.

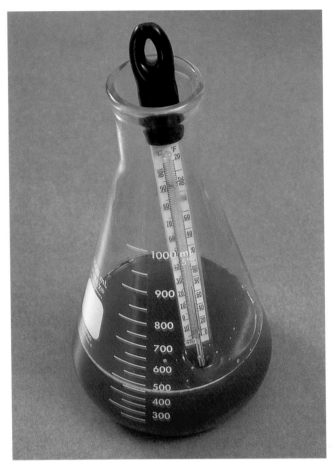

5. Cool the wort (or allow the wort to cool, depending on what method you use) to 75°F (24°C), an ideal temperature for starting a fermentation. Higher temperatures may kill the yeast. While the wort is cooling, take the yeast packet out of the refrigerator and allow it to come to room temperature as well—do not add cold yeast to warm wort!

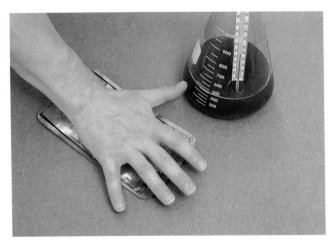

6. Smack the yeast packet to break the inner nutrient container. Shake the packet to mix the yeast with the nutrient. (If you were not making a starter culture, this is all you would need to do to activate the yeast and begin to culture it in the package.)

7. Sanitize the scissors by rubbing them with alcohol.

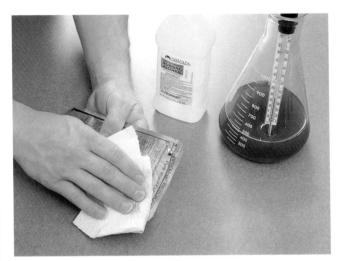

8. Do the same for the yeast packet.

9. Cut off the top of the package . . .

. . . and pour the yeast and nutrient into the wort.

10. Shake the flask to aerate the wort. Air helps the yeast feed.

11. Attach the stopper and airlock. Fill the airlock to the halfway point with a weak solution of water and sanitizer (i.e., the sanitizer should be well diluted). Maintain a temperature of 75°F (24°C). Observe the airlock for signs of fermentation: as carbon dioxide gas is produced, bubbles will emerge from the airlock. An active fermentation will produce a high krausen, or head of foam, on the wort. When this happens, usually after one or two days, your yeast is ready to be pitched, or added to the beer.

Your brewing equipment must be clean. Remove any visible dirt or debris from all surfaces that touch the beer by washing them with dish detergent or soap. Unscented soaps are best, to avoid leaving any unwanted scent on your equipment. Thoroughly rinse off any soap residues.

A long-handled brush can be used to clean the insides of glass carboys; this process is much easier if done immediately after the carboys are emptied.

Because invisible microorganisms can live on surfaces that appear clean and can infect and ruin your beer, *all brewing equipment that touches the beer also should be sanitized.* Ignoring this warning can result in a host of problems with your beer, including sourness, cloudiness, overcarbonation, and even surface mold.

Sanitizing differs from sterilization. Sterilization kills all microorganisms and would be ideal, but because certain microorganisms can survive even boiling temperatures, true sterilization can be achieved only with special laboratory equipment. For the beginner, the easiest way to sanitize equipment is to either boil it or soak it in a mild bleach solution. Boiling the wort in your brew kettle will sanitize it, and it's also best to boil wort chillers in the beer before using them.

For other equipment, make a solution of 1 to 2 ounces of household bleach in 5 gallons of cold water. Before brewing, fill your fermenters with this solution and drop in the other equipment. Let it soak for half an hour. Take the time to make sure the solution goes inside your siphon hoses.

After you've soaked your gear, you can rinse off any chlorine aroma with tap water, provided the water is drinkable. The chance of reintroducing any microorganisms from your tap is very small.

Iodine solutions such as iodophor are also highly effective (and legally registered) sanitizers. Two teaspoons in a 5-gallon container will effectively sanitize equipment in ten minutes.

Weaker solutions won't require rinsing, although you should do so if you notice a residual aroma or color on your equipment.

Other over-the-counter products, including One-Step (which produces hydrogen peroxide) and liquid acid sanitizers such as Star San, also can be effective. Follow the package directions.

Your fermenting yeast is bubbling away and you're ready to brew. You've got the necessary equipment and ingredients on hand as listed below. Time to get to it!

Equipment Needed

- ☐ boiling kettle
- ☐ kitchen pot for warming extract
- ☐ stainless-steel spoon
- ☐ thermometer
- ☐ hydrometer
- ☐ kitchen baster
- ☐ kitchen whisk
- ☐ strainer or cheesecloth and bungee cord
- ☐ hops sacks and clips or clothespins
- ☐ plastic fermenter
- ☐ rubber cork
- ☐ 3 to 4 feet of plastic tubing
- ☐ ice and/or ice packs
- ☐ glass jar with water and sanitizer

Ingredients Needed

- ☐ tap water
- ☐ malt extract
- ☐ hops
- ☐ yeast starter culture
- ☐ Irish moss (optional)

1. As early in the day as you can, boil and refrigerate 2 gallons of cooling water. (If you have a 5-gallon kettle, you can skip this step.) If you have a 4-gallon brew kettle (which will allow you to make 3 gallons of wort), you will need to add the 2 gallons of water later to make a 5-gallon batch before you pitch the yeast.

Boil for at least 5 minutes, then transfer this water to another container and cool it in your refrigerator (or outside, if it's winter). Technically, water must be heated to temperatures above the boiling point to kill *all* the bacteria in it, but this method works.

2. Before you can brew, you must sanitize all equipment that will touch the wort after boiling. The tubing, cork, thermometer, hydrometer, baster, whisk, and strainer all can be put in the secondary fermenter. Don't forget to sanitize the lid of the plastic fermenter.

3. Warming the malt extract is a good idea to make it thin enough to pour. Submerging it in very hot tap water usually does the trick, or you can boil extra water when you're making your cooling water. If you're using cans of extract, open them first with a can opener before warming them.

4. To start the actual boil, fill the brew kettle with 3½ gallons of water (the extra will allow for boil-off) and heat to 180°F (82°C).

5. Switch off the stove and stir in the malt extract. Leaving the burner or flame on may cause the extract to caramelize and burn, as it often sticks to the bottom of the kettle. After the extract has dissolved, bring the wort to a low boil.

6. Note the time and add the bittering hops. This recipe calls for 0.5 ounce of Northern Brewer, added in pellet form directly to the wort. This will be the start of a 60-minute boil. Be careful not to let the wort boil over, and use a low flame to prevent it from scorching.

7. At 30 minutes into the boil, add the flavoring hops. This recipe calls for 0.5 ounce of Willamette, added directly to the boil in plug form.

A neater method for adding the hops is to place them in a mesh hops sack and clip it to the side of the kettle.

Hops sacks can be knotted and dropped into the kettle as well, but since they are reusable, tie them loosely.

8. At 50 minutes into the boil, add the aroma hops, another 0.5 ounce of Willamette. This photo shows the addition of whole-leaf hops directly into the boil. Also add the Irish moss, if you're using it: $^1/_4$ to $^1/_2$ teaspoon for a 5-gallon batch. The most effective way to add it is to rehydrate it first in a little water. Turn off the stove after 60 minutes.

9. Chill the wort as quickly as you can. The ultimate goal is to bring the temperature down to 75°F (24°C) so you can add the yeast. (Adding your cooling water will also help with this process.) Place the kettle in a sink or tub filled with ice water (you can add a couple ice packs) or outside, if there's snow. If you've bought a wort chiller, this is the time to use it. (See Chapter 3 for photos of wort chilling in action.)

10. After the wort has cooled, strain it into the primary fermenter. You can use a new cheesecloth attached with a bungee cord, or a large kitchen strainer or colander. (Make sure you've sanitized it!)

11. Add the cooling water to help with the chilling process. Leave an inch or two of space in the top of the fermenter to allow room for foaming as the yeast becomes active. A 6-gallon fermenter gives plenty of extra room.

content. Make sure the temperature is close to 75°F (24°C), the right range for yeast pitching. Lower temperatures, down to 60°F (16°C), are acceptable, but higher temperatures may kill the yeast. If the wort temperature is still too high, you need to wait for it to cool.

13. Use the baster to fill the hydrometer tube with the wort. The hydrometer's measurement of the liquid's density will help you determine how much alcohol your wort has the potential to produce. During fermentation, as the yeast converts the sugar to alcohol, the density of the liquid drops.

12. Check and make a note of the wort temperature. You'll need this information when you take a specific gravity reading to help determine your beer's alcohol

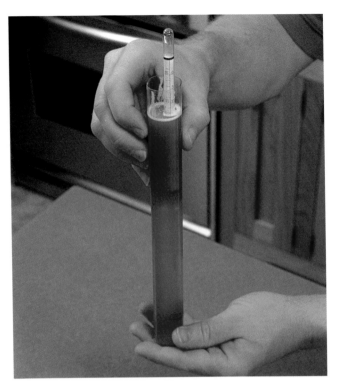

14. Fill the tube to the point at which the hydrometer floats. Spin the hydrometer in the tube to dislodge any bubbles from it (these make it float higher). Read the figure where the surface of the liquid cuts across the stem of the hydrometer.

To obtain a correct original specific gravity (OG) reading, you may have to adjust for temperature. (See the "Specific Gravity Measurements and the Hydrometer" sidebar and the instructions that came with your hydrometer for more details on taking readings.) Discard or drink the wort sample after testing; do not return it to the fermenter!

15. Aerating the wort helps the yeast work faster. You can whisk the wort, although some brewers cover the fermenter tightly and shake it. Either method slightly increases the risk of introducing airborne bacteria into the wort. A more advanced aeration method involves bubbling oxygen through the wort with an aquarium pump and aeration stone, which creates very small bubbles.

16. Pitch (pour) the yeast slurry, or mixture, into the wort. The yeast culture should be actively foaming (called "at high krausen") when it is pitched.

17. Cap the fermenter tightly and attach a stopper with a blow-off hose in the center. This piece of tubing will allow the gases produced by the vigorous early stages of fermentation to escape. (Don't use an airlock, as they often become clogged by the activity at this stage of fermentation.) Place the other end of the hose in a glass jar or other container half filled with water and a bit of sanitizer such as bleach. Make sure the end of the hose is submerged. This will allow gases to bubble out without letting air in.

Keep the fermenter at 75°F (24°C) until fermentation begins. Bubbles should emerge from the hose within twenty-four hours of pitching the yeast. After fermentation has begun, the temperature can be lowered to 60 to 70°F (16 to 21°C). Congratulations—your beer is underway!

Specific Gravity Measurements and the Hydrometer

A hydrometer measures the weight or density of a liquid in relation to water. By floating the hydrometer in a liquid and reading how high it floats on a scale, you can determine how dense the liquid is. Because wort becomes less dense as sugars are converted to alcohol during fermentation, comparing before and after readings can tell you how much alcohol your brew contains.

Follow the instructions on pages 27–28 for floating the hydrometer in a sample of your wort. Spin the hydrometer to clear it of bubbles, which may make it float too high. The scale on the hydrometer is set so that water reads at 1.000. Most beers start fermentation (have an original gravity) between 1.040 and 1.070, and end fermentation (terminal or final gravity) between 1.008 and 1.015.

Read the hydrometer at the point where the wort sample crosses the stem of the glass tube. The liquid will rise where it contacts the outside sample tube, forming an artificially high meniscus. Do not read the hydrometer along this line.

Use the following table to correct your hydrometer reading for the temperature of the liquid:

Temperature (°F)	Specific gravity correction
50	subtract .0005
60	no correction
70	add .001
77	add .002
84	add .003
95	add .005
105	add .007

For example, if your sample of Parker's Amber Ale wort is at 70°F (21°C) before you pitch the yeast, and you read 1.045 on the hydrometer, add .001 to get a corrected reading of 1.046.

Subtract the final gravity from the original gravity, and multiply that figure by 105 to determine the alcohol content of the beer. If, for example, your final reading after fermentation is 1.010, then 1.046 (original gravity) minus 1.010 (final gravity) equals 0.036. Multiplying that by 105 gives you an alcohol content of 3.78 percent by weight. This times 1.25 gives you 4.725 percent alcohol by volume.

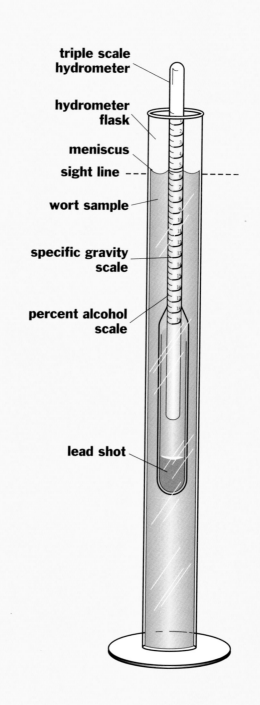

triple scale hydrometer

hydrometer flask

meniscus

sight line

wort sample

specific gravity scale

percent alcohol scale

lead shot

Basic Techniques

If you have a triple scale hydrometer, you can also use its percent alcohol scale to determine alcohol content. Subtract the original percent alcohol reading from the final percent alcohol reading to determine percent alcohol by volume.

During the first two days after you brew, you should notice an active fermentation in the primary fermenter. Bubbles emerge regularly from the hose, and a brownish foam (the krausen) may emerge also. Keep an eye on the fermenter and replace the lid if it loosens! After this activity subsides—usually two to three days after the yeast was pitched—transfer the beer to a secondary glass fermenter.

Although this step is not one hundred percent necessary to create a good beer, it will definitely improve the quality of your brew. The initial stage of fermentation produces not only the bitter hops-tinged foam on the surface of the beer, but also spent yeast that settles to the bottom. Removing the fermenting wort from these two substances can reduce off flavors.

Equipment Needed

- [ ] plastic racking cane
- [ ] 3 to 4 feet of rubber siphon hose
- [ ] glass carboy
- [ ] drilled rubber cork
- [ ] airlock
- [ ] sanitizing container

Ingredients Needed

- [ ] none

1. As always, your first priority should be cleanliness. Fill the fermenter with a sanitizing solution and submerge the racking cane most of the way into it. Sanitize the rest of the equipment, including the rubber siphon tube, in a separate container.

2. The procedure for transferring the beer involves siphoning it from the primary fermenter into the secondary. (See the "Siphoning Tips" sidebar on the next page.) To start a siphon, place the secondary fermenter below the primary, such that the level of the liquid in it will not rise above the level of the liquid in the primary fermenter.

Attach the plastic tubing to the bent end of the racking cane, and fill the tube and cane with water. Boiled water is best, but tap water will do. Pinch the end of the rubber hose (in the left hand, in the photo) to keep the water from running out of the racking cane (held in the right hand).

3. Next, plunge the free end of the racking cane into the beer in the primary fermenter. Then release the pinch grip on the rubber hose while you insert it into the glass carboy (secondary fermenter). The water will flow out of the rubber hose into the secondary fermenter, drawing beer from the primary fermenter along with it.

Keep the tip of the racking cane beneath the surface of the beer in the primary fermenter. If air enters the tube, the siphon action will stop. The plastic cap on the end of the racking cane should prevent spent yeast at the bottom of the fermenter from being sucked into the tube.

If you've used a primary fermenter that has a plastic draincock (see the bottling bucket on page 35), you can avoid siphoning by attaching the rubber tubing directly to the draincock and draining the wort into the secondary fermenter.

4. Attach a stopper and airlock to the secondary fermenter. As you did with the yeast starter culture, fill the airlock halfway with a water-and-sanitizer solution. For this ale yeast, keep the fermenter at room temperature, 60 to 70°F (16 to 21°C), and out of direct sunlight. The fermenter should show signs of yeast activity, bubbling at the airlock, for several days.

5. You'll find that spent yeast sediment typically collects at the bottom of the empty primary fermenter.

Siphoning Tips

Siphoning can be tricky. You can often avoid it by using fermentation and bottling buckets with drain spouts near the bottom. Siphoning relies on atmospheric pressure acting on the surface of the liquid, and thus the weight of the liquid itself, to force it up and through a hose that has one end placed in the liquid and the other in another vessel. Here are some tips for successful siphoning:

- The exit end of the siphon hose *must remain below* the surface of the liquid in the container from which the siphon originates, or the flow will stop. As the exit end of the tube is lowered, the rate of flow will increase. You can raise the exit end of the siphon hose above the level of the liquid to temporarily stop the flow.

- Start a siphon by initiating a flow through the hose. Fill the hose with liquid, place one end in the liquid to be siphoned, and then release the other end to start the flow by gravity. Sucking on a siphon hose to start it is possible, but this is unsanitary and can be very difficult. Special siphon-starting pumps are available.

- Keep a siphon going by ensuring that the entrance end of the hose remains below the surface of the liquid being siphoned. If an air bubble gets into the hose, it will rise to the highest point and block the siphon.

- The entrance end of the siphon hose can be placed at any level in the liquid being siphoned. If this end of the hose is outfitted with a plastic cap, such as those attached to racking canes, the end can be placed and left on the bottom of the fermenter without fear of sucking up yeast sediment and clogging the hose.

The question of when the fermentation is complete is not critical. Beer can be stored in the fermenter, with an active airlock, for up to a month without deteriorating. This is especially true if you have transferred the beer to a secondary fermenter, getting it off of the initial spent yeast.

Most of the fermentation activity will stop six to twelve days after you have transferred the beer—the airlock will stop bubbling. The remaining yeast will settle to the bottom, and the beer may begin to clear a bit. You can also confirm that fermentation is complete by taking hydrometer readings of the beer on successive days. Unchanged readings indicate a completed fermentation. At this point, the beer is ready to be bottled.

Equipment Needed

- [ ] about fifty-three 12-ounce bottles
- [ ] bottle capper
- [ ] bottle brush
- [ ] water-jet bottle cleaner (optional)
- [ ] kitchen baster
- [ ] hydrometer
- [ ] small kitchen pan
- [ ] stainless-steel spoon
- [ ] measuring cup
- [ ] bottling bucket (primary fermenter can be used)
- [ ] rubber tubing
- [ ] plastic bottle filler (optional)
- [ ] picnic cooler (optional)

Ingredients Needed

- [ ] priming (corn) sugar
- [ ] tap water

1. By far the most time-consuming aspect of bottling your beer is cleaning the bottles. If you've kept them clean after previous use, you'll be in good shape. But if mold or other fungi have developed in the bottom of the bottles, this will need to be scrubbed out and the bottles sanitized before you can use them. Scrub your bottles with a wire bottle brush . . .

Basic Techniques

... and rinse with a water-jet washer, which screws onto the kitchen faucet with a hose-fitting adapter. Pressing the bottle down onto the valve releases a forceful jet of water into the bottle.

2. A good technique for sanitizing the bottles and bottling equipment is to immerse everything in a large picnic cooler filled with sanitizing solution. Bottles have to be dunked one at a time to get the air out of them and should be rinsed afterward if bleach is used. The caps can be floated underwater in a plastic container (as here) or boiled in a pan on the stove.

3. If you haven't already done so, take a hydrometer reading to determine the final specific gravity (FG) of your beer. This reading can be used to determine the alcohol content of the finished product. (See the "Specific Gravity Measurements and the Hydrometer" sidebar for more details.)

5. Priming sugar (usually corn sugar) is added to the beer before it is bottled to induce a small secondary fermentation, which carbonates the beer in the bottles. The yeast is reactivated by the addition of the extra sugar, producing carbon dioxide that stays in solution in the beer. Make a priming sugar solution by boiling a pint of water and adding $3/4$ cup of priming sugar.

4. Siphon the beer from the secondary fermenter into a bottling bucket. (See the "Siphoning Tips" sidebar.) This step is optional but has several advantages. First, you can remove the beer from the remaining yeast sediment in one neat step rather than as you bottle, which can stir up and recirculate the sediment. Second, you can easily add priming sugar to the beer in the bottling bucket, stirring it freely without concern about raising the yeast sediment. (Small amounts of sugar can be added to individual bottles, but this is a more time-consuming and exacting proposition.) Finally, you can use a bottling bucket that has a draincock, which allows you to bottle without starting and stopping a siphon.

6. Cool the solution slightly, then stir it into the bottling bucket. The solution should not be boiling, but it can still be very warm, as this small amount of liquid will not affect the overall temperature of the beer.

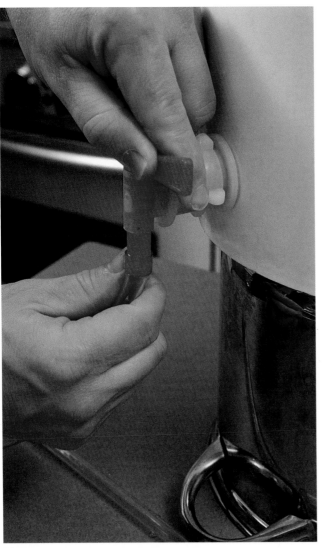

7. Elevate the bottling bucket slightly (here it's resting on an upside-down kettle) and attach the rubber hose to the draincock. Connect the other end of the rubber hose to the bottle filler (a plastic pipette with a valve on one end).

8. Open the draincock and press the tip of the bottle filler down inside the bottle to fill it neatly. Leave about an inch of space at the top of each bottle.

9. Place a cap on top of the bottle.

To use a benchtop bottle capper, slide the bottling lever up or down to adjust its height, then place the bottle under the handle and press down.

Bottled ales will require about seven to fourteen days to carbonate and age properly before they are drinkable. Store the bottles at a temperature between 55 and 70°F (13 and 70°C). Chill a bottle and test it after a week!

10. To use a wing-type bottle capper, place the capper on top of the bottle, and press down firmly on the handles.

3

Wort Chilling and Dry Hopping
Paradise Pale Ale

Pale ales have more hops and are higher in alcohol content than English bitters such as Parker's Amber Ale. They are sometimes brewed with water that contains a high mineral content, which gives the beer a drier character. Pale ales are popular among American microbrewers; Sierra Nevada Pale Ale is among the most well known. Bass Ale, Whitbread's Pale Ale, and Samuel Smith's Pale Ale are among the better-known British imports.

India pale ales are among the most highly hopped and bitter of brews. They were originally exported from England to its colonies in India. The beer's high hops content helped preserve it during the long sea journey. The Anchor Brewing Company's Liberty Ale and Ballantine's India Pale Ale are examples.

Like other ales, pale ale is made with a top-fermenting yeast, which often temporarily gathers at the top of the container during fermentation before settling to the bottom. It is fermented between 55 and 70°F (13 and 21°C).

In this chapter, as you brew a pale ale, you'll learn about wort chillers and wort chilling, as well as dry hopping. Wort chilling, or quickly cooling the wort after the boil, is one of the most important techniques for improving the quality of your beer, for several reasons. First, it reduces the time between boiling the wort and pitching the yeast, when the wort can become contaminated with microorganisms. Rapid cooling of the wort also causes solids—called the cold break—to form and fall out of solution. When the beer is transferred to the

Ingredients

- [ ] 4 pounds light liquid malt extract
- [ ] 2 pounds light dry malt extract
- [ ] 0.5 ounce Chinook hops, 60 minutes
- [ ] 0.5 ounce Chinook hops, 30 minutes
- [ ] 0.5 ounce Cascade hops, 10 minutes
- [ ] 1 ounce Cascade hops (whole) for dry hopping
- [ ] Wyeast 1332, Northwest Ale yeast
- [ ] priming sugar for bottling

Optional

- [ ] dry malt extract for the yeast starter culture
- [ ] 0.5 teaspoon Irish moss (add during last 10 minutes of boil)
- [ ] 1–4 teaspoons gypsum, or calcium sulfate (add at beginning of boil)

Why, if 'tis dancing you would be
There's brisker pipes than poetry.
Say, for what were hop-yards meant,
Or why was Burton built on Trent?
Oh, many a peer of England brews
Livelier liquor than the Muse,
And malt does more than Milton can
To justify God's ways to man.
Ale, man, ale's the stuff to drink
For fellows whom it hurts to think:
Look into the pewter pot
To see the world as the world's not.
And faith, 'tis pleasant till 'tis past:
The mischief is that 'twill not last.

—Excerpt from "Shropshire Lad #62,"
A. E. Housman

Ingredient Timing

:00	Boil begins Add 0.5 ounce Chinook hops Add gypsum (optional)
:30	Add another 0.5 ounce Chinook hops
:50	Add 0.5 ounce Cascade hops Insert copper immersion wort chiller Add 0.5 teaspoon Irish moss (optional)
:60	Remove from heat

Original specific gravity:	**1.052**
Final specific gravity	**1.010**

fermenter, these solids are left behind, clarifying the beer. Finally, wort chilling slows the production of dimethyl sulfide (DMS), which can give a cooked-corn aroma to beer. This chapter illustrates the use of a coiled copper-tubing immersion chiller, probably the most common type, but others are described as well.

Dry hopping is the technique of adding loose, dry hops to the wort during fermentation. This adds a distinct hops aroma to the beer, one of the characteristics of the pale ale style.

About Paradise Pale Ale

Paradise Pale Ale may have been named after the region of the United States where the Cascade hops it uses are grown: the Pacific Northwest. Cascade is one of the most distinctive American hops varieties, and it gives Sierra Nevada's beers their characteristic nose. Paradise Pale Ale also uses Northwest Ale yeast, which produces a malty and mildly fruity ale. The original specific gravity is slightly higher than that of Parker's Amber Ale, indicating a higher potential alcohol content.

Start the yeast culture two days in advance of brewing. The Wyeast Activator does not need to be cultured and can be used within hours of its activation. Follow the directions on the package.

On brew day, follow the same steps as for the Amber Ale: After sanitizing your equipment, heat the water to 180°F (82°C), and stir in the dried malt extract along with the liquid extract. If you decide to add gypsum to this beer, do so at the beginning of the boil. You can base this decision on your water hardness, keeping in mind that malt extracts often contain water-hardening minerals.

You add 0.5 ounce of the Chinook hops at the beginning of the boil, another 0.5 ounce halfway through, and a final 0.5 ounce with 10 minutes left in the boil, along with the Irish moss if desired.

Wort Chilling

1. Place the copper immersion wort chiller in the boiling wort for the final 10 minutes. This will sterilize the wort chiller.

2. After the boil is over, switch off the stove and transfer the kettle to the sink. The wort chiller inlet hose can be connected to the sink faucet with a garden-hose adapter.

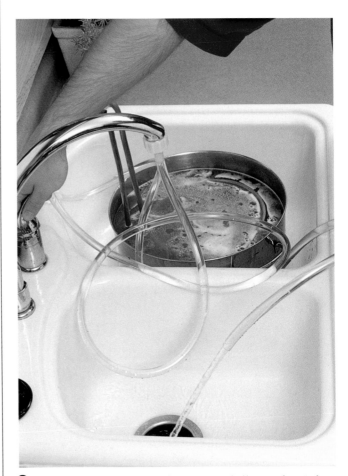

3. Place the outlet hose of the wort chiller in the sink drain and turn on the faucet to allow cold water to flow through the chiller. Turn the water on slowly and only partially to prevent leaks from developing in the chiller hose fittings. High pressure is not necessary to cool the wort and may cause a hose to pop off.

4. As the wort chiller cools the beer, check it occasionally with the sanitized thermometer. Cool it to 75°F (24°C) for yeast pitching. If you're adding cooling water, take this into consideration as you bring the temperature down.

5. After the wort has been cooled, remove the chiller and cover the pot to prevent contamination. Remove the faucet adapter from the faucet.

Dry Hopping

1. When you are ready to transfer the wort to the secondary fermenter, dry-hop the beer by adding the remaining hops (1 ounce of Cascade) to the empty fermenter. Use whole hops flowers for this step.

One concern with dry hopping is the risk of contaminating the beer with the hops. To reduce this risk, prolong the primary fermentation by a day or two before the transfer. This increases the alcohol content of the wort, which will help kill bacteria that might be introduced by the hops.

The hops also can be placed in a mesh sack and added to the carboy.

2. When the beer is siphoned from the primary fermenter into the secondary, the loose hops will float to the top, but they should then sink down after they have become saturated.

Allow the beer to sit on the hops for at least a week. When you rack the beer (transfer it into a bottling container), you'll leave the hops behind in the glass carboy. If you're kegging your beer, you can pour it into the keg through a cheesecloth or strainer.

Wort Chillers

Wort chillers come in many varieties, including immersion and counterflow chillers. They can be made quite easily.

The basic copper immersion chiller is simply a 25-foot coil of copper tubing (known as soft copper to plumbers) with hoses attached at each end. To bend soft copper tubing into a large spiral, wrap it around an object such as a one-gallon paint can. This will prevent kinking or breaking the copper. Make sure the coil will fit inside your brew kettle. To make the hose attachments at the ends, use a tube bender, a spiraled coil of wire that is placed around the copper tubing so that you can bend it easily. Attach the lengths of rubber tubing with metal hose clamps.

The counterflow chiller circulates the hot wort in one direction through a copper tube and cold water in the opposite direction through a larger tube or container surrounding the copper. It has been mathematically demonstrated that this type of chiller is more

effective than the immersion chiller, but it is more complicated to make.

One type can be made by inserting a section of copper tubing into the center of a garden hose (see photo on page 14). Straighten the length of copper and grease it with petroleum jelly before threading it through the hose. After the copper has been inserted in the hose, coil the assembly and make two end caps for the chiller from copper plumbing Ts (some soldering is required). These end caps enable you to circulate water through the hose at the same time that the wort is circulated through the copper.

A counterflow chiller is more difficult to clean, as the wort circulates inside it. To effectively clean it, flow hot water through the wort tubing immediately after use. This will remove most wort residue. Before using the chiller again, run water through the wort tubing, leaving it full, then submerge the chiller in a kettle of water and bring to a boil. This will also boil the water inside the chiller.

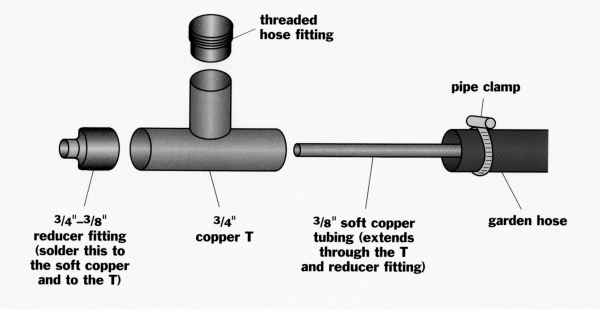

threaded hose fitting

pipe clamp

3/4"–3/8" reducer fitting (solder this to the soft copper and to the T)

3/4" copper T

3/8" soft copper tubing (extends through the T and reducer fitting)

garden hose

4

Using Specialty Grains
Parliamentary Porter

The porter is a classic traditional British ale style. Porters are characterized by their dark color, although they don't have to be excessively full-bodied. Their alcohol content is not as high as a stout, and they were once considered to be the drink of the common man. As such, they were often homebrewed. Good porters in the United States are brewed by Anchor, Sierra Nevada, Troegs, and Brooklyn brewing companies.

About Parliamentary Porter
Parliamentary Porter's dark color comes from steeping cracked, dark-roasted grains in hot water before the boil. This technique introduces you to the use and handling of specialty grains, which can add distinct flavors to beers. Medium-colored crystal malts and dark-colored roasted malts have had much of their starches converted to sugar by the malting process. As a result, they require only a short period of steeping to produce usable sugar and color in the wort. Lighter-colored grains such as two-row malts need to undergo the process of mashing, or the conversion of starch to sugar, before they can be used in beer.

The base for the Parliamentary Porter is a light extract, which allows you to clearly see the effect of steeping the grains. It uses two dark-roasted malts—chocolate and black barley—which are readily available from homebrew suppliers. Briess is a reputable brand, as are

Ingredients

- ☐ 7 pounds light liquid malt extract
- ☐ 0.5 pound Briess chocolate malt
- ☐ 0.5 pound Briess black barley malt
- ☐ 1 ounce Kent Goldings hops, 60 minutes
- ☐ 0.5 ounce Kent Goldings hops, 30 minutes
- ☐ 1 ounce Fuggles hops, 15 minutes
- ☐ 0.5 ounce Fuggles hops, 5 minutes
- ☐ Wyeast 1084, Irish Ale yeast
- ☐ priming sugar for bottling

Optional

- ☐ dry malt extract for the yeast starter culture
- ☐ 0.5 teaspoon Irish moss (add during last 10 minutes of boil)

John Barleycorn was a hero bold,
Of noble enterprise;
For if you do but taste his blood,
'Twill make your courage rise.
'Twill make a man forget his woe;
'Twill heighten all his joy;
'Twill make the widow's heart to sing,
Tho' the tear were in her eye.
Then let us toast John Barleycorn,
Each man a glass in hand;
And may his great posterity
Ne'er fail in old Scotland!

—"John Barleycorn," Robert Burns

Ingredient Timing

:00	Boil begins Add 1 ounce Kent Goldings hops
:30	Add another 0.5 ounce Kent Goldings hops
:45	Add 1 ounce Fuggles hops
:50	Add 0.5 teaspoon Irish moss (optional)
:55	Add 0.5 ounce Fuggles hops
:60	Remove from heat

Original specific gravity:	**1.057**
Final specific gravity:	**1.012**

Durst, Dingemans, Weyermann, and Munton and Fison. The hops are both traditional, relatively low-acidity British varieties: Fuggles and Kent Goldings.

As with other ales, porters are brewed with a top-fermenting yeast, which often temporarily gathers at the top of the container during fermentation before settling to the bottom. They are fermented between 55 and 70°F (13 and 21°C).

Start the brewing process as in the other recipes, making a yeast culture, sanitizing the equipment, and boiling and refrigerating any needed cooling water. Then use the following steps to introduce the roasted barley grains at the beginning of the boil.

1. Crack open and slightly crush the whole chocolate and black barley grains with a rolling pin. The grains can be mixed together or cracked separately.

Properly cracked grains (left) compared with uncracked grains (right). Nearly all of the hulls have been broken open, and some grains have been completely shattered.

This grain mill is attached to a board that can be placed on top of a food-grade bucket. Others are mountable on walls or benches. Adjustments to the grinding wheels can change the degree to which the grains are cracked.

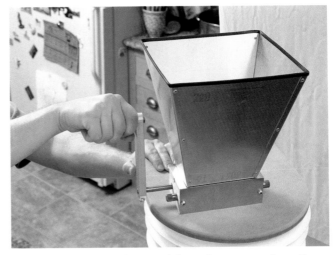

The hand crank on this model can be removed to allow the attachment of an electric drill for grinding large quantities of grains.

Using Specialty Grains

2. Place the grains in a grain sack. Tie the sack closed, or just tighten the drawstring if you plan to secure it to the side of the kettle.

3. Bring 3 gallons of water up to 165°F (74°C).

4. Add the knotted grain sack to the water and steep the grains in the water for 30 minutes.

Clipping the unknotted grain sack to the side of the kettle can make it easier to reopen the sack after steeping, when it is hot and wet.

47

5. Heat another $1/2$ gallon of water to 165°F (74°C). Place the grain bag in a shallow bowl, and rinse the grains with the heated water.

An alternative way to do this is to pour the water over and into the grain bag.

6. Discard the spent grains. You may want to compost them or add them to bread dough.

7. Add the rinse water from the grains to the wort.

8. Stir in the extract, making sure it all dissolves off the bottom of the pot. Bring the wort to a boil, and add the hops at the appropriate times as in the amber and pale ale recipes.

5

Specialty Grains and Dry Hopping
Old Bald Fart Barley Wine

Barley wines, the strongest and most alcoholic of all beers, are an unusual style. They use large quantities of malt sugar, producing a high alcohol content (usually 8 to 12 percent) and a rich, winelike flavor. Hopping rates vary. English varieties like Thomas Hardy's Ale usually use less hops than do American examples such as Sierra Nevada's Bigfoot Barley Wine and Rogue's Old Crustacean.

Although the name barley wine was first introduced by the Bass Ale Brewery relatively recently, in 1903, barley wines probably originated with an old style of brewing called parti-gyle. In this process, several beers were made from the same kettle of mash. The first wort that was drained from the steeping grains made an intensely strong beer, which became the forerunner of the barley wine. Later spargings, or rinsings, of the same grains made progressively weaker beers.

Barley wines are usually fermented with ale yeast. The yeast should be very alcohol-tolerant because of the high alcohol levels created by the fermentation process. A weaker strain of yeast might stop fermenting too early, leaving unfermented malt sugars and an undesirable sweetness in the beer.

Barley wines can be consumed with food or appetizers, and they also can be served in smaller quantities as an aperitif. They age well and can be cellared like wines. They typically lose some hops character and become drier with time.

Ingredient Timing

:00 Boil begins
Add 1 ounce Columbus hops

:15 Add 0.5 ounce Centennial hops
Add 0.5 ounce Cascade hops

:30 Add another 0.25 ounce Centennial hops
Add another 0.25 ounce Cascade hops

:50 Add 0.5 teaspoon Irish moss (optional)

:55 Add another 0.5 ounce Centennial hops
Add another 0.5 ounce Cascade hops

:60 Remove from heat

Original specific gravity:	**1.090**
Final specific gravity:	**1.016**

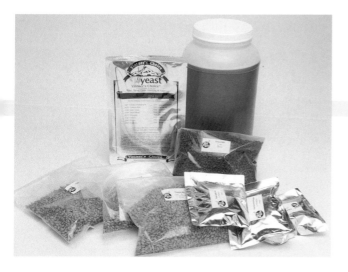

About Old Bald Fart Barley Wine

This recipe was the most popular beer at Dimmer's, a Fort Collins, Colorado, brewpub where Jim Parker was the original head brewer. Typical of barley wines, it uses a large quantity of pale malt extract, colored with some crystal and chocolate malt grains. Steep these grains in hot water before the boil as done for the Parliamentary Porter.

Make a large yeast starter culture for this beer two or three days in advance. A ¹/₂-gallon milk bottle provides a starter about 10 percent of the size of the beer batch, a recommended rate.

The hopping schedule is intense. Two relatively high-bitterness hops, Columbus and Centennial, are

"For a quart of ale is a dish for a King."

—William Shakespeare,
Winter's Tale, Act IV, Scene 2

Ingredients

- [ ] 9 pounds pale liquid malt extract
- [ ] 0.5 pound special roast malt
- [ ] 0.5 pound 40°L crystal malt
- [ ] 0.5 pound 105°L crystal malt
- [ ] 0.25 pound chocolate malt
- [ ] 1 ounce Columbus hops, 60 minutes
- [ ] 0.5 ounce Centennial hops, 45 minutes
- [ ] 0.5 ounce Cascade hops, 45 minutes
- [ ] 0.25 ounce Centennial hops, 30 minutes
- [ ] 0.25 ounce Cascade hops, 30 minutes
- [ ] 0.5 ounce Centennial hops, 5 minutes
- [ ] 0.5 ounce Cascade hops, 5 minutes
- [ ] 0.5 ounce Centennial hops, dry hop
- [ ] 0.5 ounce Cascade hops, dry hop
- [ ] Wyeast 1056, American Ale yeast
- [ ] 2 cups dry malt extract for the yeast starter culture
- [ ] priming sugar for bottling and carbonating

Optional

- [ ] 0.5 teaspoon Irish moss (add during last 10 minutes of boil)

used along with Cascade to counteract the deep maltiness of the beer. They are added throughout the boil and again during the fermentation (dry hopping) to produce a strong, aromatic hops character.

Starter Culture

Start the brewing process two or three days in advance by making a larger yeast culture (refer to Chapter 2 for instructions). Before beginning, sanitize all equipment used in the process.

1. Add 2 cups of dried malt extract to 2 quarts (¹/₂ gallon) of boiling water. Boil for 10 minutes, then allow this weak wort to cool to 70 to 75°F (21 to 24°C) and pour it into a glass milk bottle.

2. Add the liquid yeast, sanitizing the yeast package and scissors with alcohol before cutting it open. Shake the bottle to aerate the wort.

3. Attach a sanitized stopper and airlock. Fill the airlock with a weak solution of water and sanitizer. Allow the yeast to multiply and grow at 75°F (24°C) until a high krausen is reached and the culture is very actively bubbling, about two to three days. A ¹/₂-gallon-size starter culture will increase the 40 to 60 billion yeast cells provided in the Wyeast package to about 225 billion cells!

Specialty Grains

On brew day, follow the standard steps for brewing a batch of beer, including cleaning and sanitizing the equipment and boiling and refrigerating any needed cooling water.

1. As in the Parliamentary Porter recipe, you'll need to crack and steep the roasted barley grains before the boil. Use a small kitchen scale to weigh out the grains.

2. Though a rolling pin will work, a grain mill is especially effective for cracking this quantity of grains.

Weighing the grains ensures that the chocolate and crystal malts are kept in proper proportion.

You can mill the barley directly over a plastic bucket, which will collect the cracked grains.

3. Pour the grains into a large mesh sack . . .

4. Heat another ¹/₂ gallon of water to 165°F (74°C). Pour this water over the grains in the bag to rinse them . . .

. . . and clip to the side of the brew kettle. Bring 3 gallons of water up to 165°F (74°C) and steep the grains for 30 minutes.

. . . and then add this rinse water to the brew kettle. Bring the wort to a boil, switch off the heat, add the extract and the first addition of hops, then continue with the boil and the hops additions as you would for any recipe.

Dry Hopping

The dry-hopping process is very similar to that of the Paradise Pale Ale. In this photo, the loose (whole cone) Centennial and Cascade hops mixture is being added to the secondary fermenter in a mesh sack.

After the initial fermentation bubble-up, transfer the beer from the primary fermenter onto these hops, and allow it to continue to ferment for at least a week. Longer fermentations might be necessary for the barley wine; use the hydrometer and the recommended specific gravity readings in the ingredients list to check your progress.

Because of its high final alcohol content and the resulting stress on the yeast, this beer might also benefit from kegging and force carbonating (see chapter 6), rather than attempting to carbonate it in the bottles with priming sugar.

6

Using Nontraditional Ingredients and Kegging
Moo-Juice Milk Stout

Stout is a legendary brew, the national beverage of Ireland. Darkest of all beers, though not always the strongest, it has become well known in the United States thanks to the Guinness brand. Guinness makes a dry stout, which is relatively low in alcohol and has a very limited hops aroma. Most of the bitterness in this type of stout comes from dark-roasted barley.

Imperial stout is a stronger form with a high alcohol content (original gravities of 1.075 to 1.090, 7 to 9 percent alcohol) and more hops bitterness. Although stouts vary greatly in alcoholic strength, body, and sweetness,

all are top-fermented (with ale yeast) and are characterized by the taste and color of dark-roasted barley.

About Moo-Juice Milk Stout

Moo-Juice Milk Stout is somewhere between these two styles. Seven pounds of malt extract, both liquid and dried, give it a fairly high alcohol content (original gravity 1.060), and it has a similar hops character to the Parliamentary Porter. Like that beer, it features cracked, dark-roasted grains for color and flavor. Steep these grains in hot water before adding the extract, as done for the porter and barley wine.

Ingredients

- [ ] 5 pounds light liquid malt extract
- [ ] 2 pounds dark dry malt extract
- [ ] 1 pound Briess chocolate malt
- [ ] 0.5 pound Briess black barley malt
- [ ] 0.5 pound roasted barley malt
- [ ] 1 ounce Brewers Gold hops, 50 minutes
- [ ] 0.5 ounce Brewers Gold hops, 30 minutes
- [ ] 1 ounce Fuggles hops, 10 minutes
- [ ] 8 ounces powdered lactose
- [ ] Wyeast 1335, British Ale yeast II

Optional

- [ ] dry malt extract for the yeast starter culture
- [ ] 0.5 teaspoon Irish moss (add during last 10 minutes of boil)

*When money's tight and hard to get
And your horse has also ran,
When all you have is a heap of debt—
A pint of plain is your only man.
When health is bad and your heart feels
  strange,
And your face is pale and wan,
When doctors say you need a change,
A pint of plain is your only man.*

—"The Workman's Friend,"
Flann O'Brien

Ingredient Timing

:00	Boil begins Add 8 ounces powdered lactose
:10	Add 1 ounce Brewers Gold hops
:30	Add another 0.5 ounce Brewers Gold hops
:50	Add 1 ounce Fuggles hops Add 0.5 teaspoon Irish moss (optional)
:60	Remove from heat

Original specific gravity:	**1.060**
Final specific gravity:	**1.014**

The milk stout also contains dissolved lactose, or milk sugar, which gives it a fuller body and a certain sweetness. Lactose does not dissolve easily, so you need to stir it into a separate slurry, which is then returned to the main wort.

This chapter also describes the process of kegging and carbonating your beer. Many brewers prefer home kegging because it saves them more time and effort than any other process, as they no longer have to wash and fill bottles or wait for the beer to carbonate naturally.

Traditionally, certain stouts are carbonated with nitrogen, which produces a creamy, thick head with tiny bubbles. Carbon dioxide also can be used, however, and typical carbon dioxide tank can be connected easily to commercial 5-gallon soda kegs. Homebrews can be carbonated in a matter of two to three days and stored easily in the keg in a refrigerator set aside for that purpose. Serving a guest your own homebrewed draft beer from a keg may be one of life's more sublime pleasures.

Start the brewing by making a yeast culture, sanitizing the equipment, and boiling and refrigerating cooling water. Crack and steep the roasted barley before the boiling, as in the Parliamentary Porter and Old Bald Fart recipes. Steeping should be done at around 150 to 170°F (65 to 76°C). Add the liquid and dried malt extracts, then bring the wort to a boil. The lactose needs to be added before the first round of hops.

Adding Lactose Sugar

1. Use a baster to pull out a pint of boiling wort. This will be returned to the boil, so you don't have to sanitize the glass jar or 16-ounce measuring cup beforehand, though it should be clean.

2. Pour the pint of wort into a metal bowl and stir in the powdered lactose sugar.

3. Return the dissolved lactose slurry to the boiling wort, then add the first round of hops. Continue adding hops, chill the wort, pitch the yeast, and ferment at temperatures between 55 and 70°F (13 and 21°C). After the secondary fermentation is complete, it's time to transfer the beer to a keg and carbonate it.

Kegging and Carbonating

Although several products are on the market for home kegging, the Cornelius keg is by far the most commonly used. New and high-quality refurbished kegs can be ordered from several sources, including Sabco Industries in Toledo, Ohio; William's Brewing in San Leandro, California, which also sells complete carbon dioxide setups; and Beer, Beer, and More Beer, also in California. A beverage supply store might be able to sell you some of this equipment, or you can ask at a local pub for the name of a reputable bar equipment distributor.

1. Clean and sanitize the keg through the top with an angled brush. After removing any debris, fill the keg with sanitizing solution, as with the fermentation containers. Be sure to sanitize the swing-top lid as well!

Using Nontraditional Ingredients

2. Siphon the beer from the secondary fermenter into the keg (see Chapter 2 for instructions on siphoning). Making sure that the beer doesn't splash during this process will slow down oxidation.

Two valves are located on the top of the keg. One is used to add carbon dioxide to pressurize the keg, and the other to dispense the beer through a tap hose. The ball-lock valve, shown here, allows the carbon dioxide hose to be attached. This type of valve is used on many soda containers. Pulling up on the ring with the fingers releases the valve.

3. To carbonate the beer, pressurize the keg by attaching a carbon dioxide tank. First seal the keg with the swing-top lid and then connect a small carbon dioxide tank with an attached set of regulator gauges to the keg.

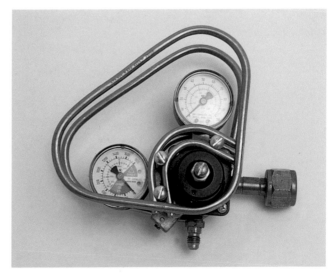

In this close-up of a carbon dioxide regulator gauge, the right-hand (upper) gauge shows the pressure in the carbon dioxide tank, and the left-hand (lower) gauge shows the amount that is being released to the keg. A set screw (center) regulates the amount of pressure that is released. The twin metal loops, fastened together with screws, form a protective cage around the dials; these are not present on all models.

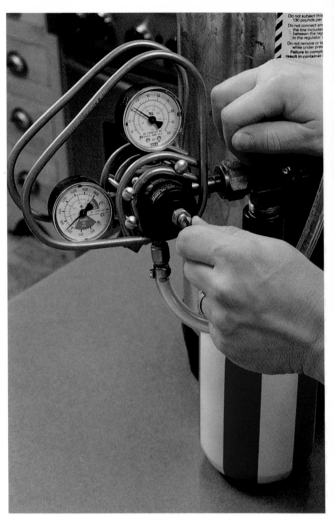

4. To pressurize the keg, first open the handle valve on top of the carbon dioxide tank. The upper dial gauge should indicate the amount of pressure in the tank.

5. Next, use a thin object such as a screwdriver or dime to adjust the set screw that regulates the amount of carbon dioxide flowing into the keg. Set this to 30 pounds per square inch (psi) to establish a steady pressurization of the keg. (See the "About Carbonation" sidebar on the next page for more information on pressure settings for obtaining desired levels of carbonation.)

6. With the carbon dioxide tank attached, pick up the keg and shake it for a minute or two to force the pressurized carbon dioxide into the beer. You can hear this happening—it's the reverse of the fizzing sound made when you open a can or bottle of your favorite beverage. Shut off the carbon dioxide and refrigerate the keg. The lowered temperature will help the carbon dioxide dissolve, and you will need less carbon dioxide to carbonate your beer at lower temperatures.

To properly carbonate the beer, repeat these steps, pressurizing and shaking the keg, twice a day for three days. You may hear less carbon dioxide escaping from the tank into the keg each time. The tank can be physically detached and reattached between each carbonation, or it can be left connected to the keg in the refrigerator with the set screw valve shut off.

After the beer has been carbonated, attach the tap hose to the second ball-lock valve on the keg, and set the carbon dioxide pressure to 8 to 10 psi for serving.

Typical refrigeration setups include an upright fridge with tap handles on the front for serving beer and a chest freezer with a Johnson temperature control unit (on the wall) connected to it. This unit cycles power on and off to the freezer to keep it at refrigerator temperatures. The tops of several kegs are visible in the freezer, and a carbon dioxide tank sits next to it.

About Carbonation

The amount of carbon dioxide dissolved in beer—its carbonation level—is measured in volumes. If a beer's carbonation level is 3 volumes, it means that every cubic inch of beer has 3 cubic inches of carbon dioxide dissolved into it at a standard temperature and pressure.

Most commercially available beers are packaged with 2.3 to 2.8 volumes of carbon dioxide. Certain beer styles differ, though, in their traditional carbonation levels. Belgian ales and German weissbiers, for example, are usually carbonated to 3 to 3.2 volumes and above. Some British ales are served at lower carbonation levels because of the limits of the wooden kegs in which they are conditioned.

To determine the pressure of carbon dioxide to use when carbonating your beer, use the table below. Find the temperature of your beer in the left column (assuming that you are carbonating it at the same temperature at which you will be serving it) and the desired volume of carbon dioxide along the top in order to determine the pressure setting to use on your carbon dioxide tank when you are force-carbonating the beer.

PRESSURES FOR CARBONATING BEER

Temp °F (°C)	Volumes of Carbon Dioxide in Solution (psi)						
	1.8	2.0	2.2	2.4	2.6	2.8	3.0
40 (4)	5	7	9	11	13	16	18
44 (7)	6	9	11	13	16	18	20
48 (9)	8	10	13	15	18	20	23
52 (11)	10	12	15	17	20	23	25
56 (13)	11	14	17	20	22	25	28

7

Lager Yeast and Lagering
Old Country Lager

The German word *lager* means "to store," and lagers are characterized by the long period of storage they undergo at cold temperatures after fermentation. This traditional German beer style is the most popular type in the world; most typical North American beers are lagers, including Budweiser, Coors, Labatts, Samuel Adams, Yuengling, Rolling Rock, and Foster's.

Lagers are brewed with a bottom-fermenting yeast, and the fermentation occurs at cooler temperatures, usually from 40 to 50°F (4.5 and 10°C). After the fermentation is complete, the beer is stored for a long period—from three weeks to three months—at temperatures below 40°F (4.5°C). This produces beers that are clean tasting and stable; at these cold temperatures, fewer esters, chemicals that can produce off flavors, develop.

Lagers are typically served cold and come in several styles, including pilsener, a very light beer with assertive hops character; Oktoberfest, a rich, copper-colored lager; bock and doppelbock, sweet, strongly alcoholic lagers with low hops content; and dry and light beers that are specially brewed to reduce calories or aftertaste.

About Old Country Lager

The Old Country Lager is a fairly typical recipe that includes some cracked barley grains. These malts are not heavily roasted and produce a lighter-colored (though not a low-alcohol) beer. The Hallertauer Hersbrucker hops is one of the varieties traditionally used in lagers, which are known collectively as noble hops. Others include Hallertauer Mittelfruh, Spalt, Saaz, and Tettnanger.

Ingredients

- [ ] 4 pounds light liquid malt extract
- [ ] 2 pounds light dry malt extract
- [ ] 0.5 pound dark Munich malt
- [ ] 0.5 pound Vienna malt
- [ ] 0.5 pound two-row malt
- [ ] 0.5 ounce Perle hops, 50 minutes
- [ ] 0.5 ounce Hallertauer Hersbrucker hops, 30 minutes
- [ ] 0.5 ounce Hallertauer Hersbrucker hops, 10 minutes
- [ ] Wyeast 2206, Bavarian Lager yeast

Optional

- [ ] dry malt extract for the yeast starter culture
- [ ] 0.5 teaspoon Irish moss (add during last 10 minutes of boil)

Ingredient Timing

:00 Boil begins

:10 Add 0.5 ounce Perle hops

:30 Add 0.5 ounce Hallertauer Hersbrucker hops

:50 Add another 0.5 ounce Hallertauer Hersbrucker hops
Add 0.5 teaspoon Irish moss (optional)

:60 Remove from heat

Original specific gravity:	**1.050**
Final specific gravity:	**1.010**

Start the brewing process as in the other recipes by making a yeast culture, sanitizing the equipment, and boiling and refrigerating any needed cooling water.

Crack and steep the roasted barley grains at 150 to 170°F (65 to 76°C) before beginning the boil, as done for the Parliamentary Porter and Moo-Juice Milk Stout recipes. The grains used in this recipe were roasted less and thus are lighter in color.

Add the liquid and dried malt extract, then bring the wort to a boil. Add the hops according to the schedule in the ingredients list.

Add the lager yeast directly to the primary fermenter, with the wort temperature around 70°F (21°C). This is the same temperature at which ale yeast is added, and it will serve to start the fermentation.

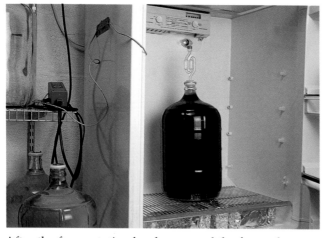

After the fermentation has begun and the foamy krausen has formed and settled down a bit, transfer the wort to a secondary fermenter and bring the temperature down to 50°F (10°C). This can be accomplished by moving the fermenter into a 50°F room, such as an unheated basement, or a temperature-controlled refrigerator.

An electronic temperature controller connected to the refrigerator can be set to maintain specific temperatures. Higher-quality models will hold the refrigerator at a steady temperature without continual on-off cycling, which can damage it.

Ferment the beer at 50°F (10°C) for ten to fourteen days, until the correct final specific gravity has been reached, at which time fermentation is essentially complete. Once this has happened, bring the temperature down to 33°F (0.5°C)—just above freezing—and allow the beer to lager in the fermenter for three to five weeks before kegging or bottling.

Lager Yeast and Lagering

8

The Minimash
Wedding Wit

Witbier, or white beer, is a traditional Belgian beer style. It is characterized by a cloudy whitish haze, which is produced by using unmalted wheat as a base malt in addition to barley. In this regard, it resembles the German hefeweizen, or wheat beer, style.

Witbiers, however, also traditionally include spices in the boil—usually coriander and orange peel, as well as other spices that are trade secrets. The Wedding Wit uses one of these. White beers are lightly hopped, and the result of this blend is a unique pale, golden, tart, and refreshing light beer. Witbiers are great for summer quaffing with light foods.

The traditional brewing center of this style was a region east of Brussels in Belgium, around the towns of Louvain and Hoegaarden. The popularity of German lagers, however, had driven the style into near extinction by the 1960s, when Pierre Celis revived it and eventually moved to Texas, establishing the Celis brewery there. Two of his commercially available products are Hoegaarden White and Celis White. Blue Moon is another popular witbier.

About Wedding Wit
This recipe is a variation of one that brewer Jim Parker developed for his wedding. In many ways, this is a typical witbier, using pale barley malt extract and wheat extract as base malts. To these are added an infusion made from mashing pilsener malt, unmalted flaked wheat, and flaked oats. Saaz hops is a mild choice, giving this beer a low bitterness. Orange peel, coriander, and grains

He that buys land buys many stones,
He that buys flesh buys many bones,
He that buys eggs buys many shells,
But he that buys good ale buys nothing
*   else.*

—Anonymous

Ingredients

- [ ] 2 pounds pale liquid malt extract
- [ ] 2 pounds wheat dried malt extract
- [ ] 2 pounds pilsener malt
- [ ] 0.5 pound unmalted flaked white wheat
- [ ] 0.5 pound flaked oats
- [ ] 1 ounce Saaz hops, 50 minutes
- [ ] 0.5 ounce fresh ground coriander, 15 minutes
- [ ] 0.5 ounce grated sweet orange peel, 15 minutes
- [ ] 0.25 ounce crushed grains of paradise, 15 minutes
- [ ] White Labs WLP400, Belgian Witbier yeast

Optional

- [ ] 0.5 teaspoon Irish moss (add during last 10 minutes of boil)

Ingredient Timing

:00	Boil begins
:10	Add 1 ounce Saaz hops
:45	Add 0.5 ounce fresh ground coriander Add 0.5 ounce grated sweet orange peel Add 0.25 ounce crushed grains of paradise
:50	Add 0.5 teaspoon Irish moss (optional)
:60	Remove from heat

Original specific gravity:	**1.043**
Final specific gravity:	**1.010**

of paradise (the secret ingredient) round out this recipe. Grains of paradise are the hot, spicy seeds of a plant in the ginger family that is native to the west coast of Africa. They look like small peppercorns and were once substituted widely for black pepper in Europe.

The process of mashing is introduced here in a simplified, single-stage stovetop procedure. The flaked grains have been pregelatinized, which breaks down their starches, allowing enzymes in the pilsener malt to convert them into sugars during the mash. Advanced brewers who want to brew entirely from grains can expand their mashing setups to allow for the processing of large quantities of malt. More complex mashing systems and processes are briefly explained in chapter 9. For this recipe, you simply soak the grains for a specified time and rinse them with hot water, adding the results to your boiling kettle.

Follow the standard steps for brewing a batch of beer, including making a yeast starter culture in advance, cleaning and sanitizing the equipment, and boiling and refrigerating any needed cooling water.

Stovetop Mashing

To conduct a minimash, begin by bringing 4.5 quarts of water up to 165°F (74°C) in a separate pot from your boiling kettle.

1. As you did for the porter and barley wine recipes, crack the pilsener malt grains using either a rolling pin or grain mill.

2. Add the cracked malt, flaked oats, and wheat to the hot water. Stir them in, intermixing them well.

3. The temperature of this mash should be about 152°F (66°C). Maintain this temperature for 45 minutes to 1 hour, either on the stovetop (being careful not to scorch the mash) . . .

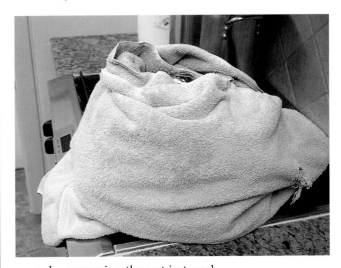

. . . or by wrapping the pot in towels.

4. Near the end of this mash, heat another 6 1/2 quarts of water to about 170°F (76°C). This will be your sparge, or rinse, water.

The Minimash

8. Add the spices with 15 minutes left in the boil. Measure out the seeds with a kitchen scale . . .

5. Secure a section of cheesecloth over the top of your boiling kettle with a large bungee cord, or place a mesh strainer or fine-holed colander onto the top. Carefully transfer your mash into the cheesecloth or strainer.

. . . and pulverize them with a mortar and pestle.

6. Slowly pour the sparge water over the minimash to rinse the sweet wort from the spent grains.

7. Compost the grains, remove the cheesecloth from the kettle, and add enough water to the brew kettle to bring the volume up to your normal boiling volume. Heat the mixture to near boiling, switch off the heat, add the malt extract, and continue as with the previous beers. Witbiers have subdued hops character, so only one addition of hops is called for, early in the boil.

9. Your spices go in a mesh hops sack that can be clipped to the side of the kettle and dropped right into the boiling wort.

Finish off the beer by adding the Irish moss with 10 minutes left in the boil. Chill the wort and transfer it to a primary fermenter as done for the other ales.

9

Introduction to Advanced Setups and Techniques

Full Mashing

Partial mashes, like the one used to make the Wedding Wit, produce a gallon or two of wort, which is then supplemented with extract. Professional brewers or advanced homebrewers who want to stop using malt extracts altogether often begin their brewing process with a full mash, using a base malt of partially cracked barley grains. The process includes striking a bed of cracked grain with initial hot water (pouring the water into the grain), allowing it to soak, draining off some wort and repouring (recirculating) it back over the grain bed to clarify and filter it, then sparging, or draining off final wort while adding fresh hot water to the top of the grain bed.

As with the partial mash, full mashing requires the ability to hold a quantity of soaking grains at a specific temperature, usually 148 to 162°F (64 to 72°C). Larger quantities of grains sufficient to produce a full 5-gallon batch of wort require larger quantities of water, up to 10 gallons, and bigger mashing kettles, called tuns.

Various home-mashing setups have been devised over the years. These include picnic coolers with frameworks of slotted or perforated pipes inside, or perforated metal false bottoms that can be placed inside kettles or insulated beverage coolers to allow liquid to drain out of them when they are filled with steeping grains.

In this mashing setup, a 10-gallon kettle is equipped with a thermometer, a drainpipe for removing wort,

and a large, circular, perforated false bottom (leaning on the left). The spiral copper pipe with holes drilled in it can be suspended over the grain bed and used to sprinkle hot water during the sparging process.

If you are interested in learning how to mash, consult one of the more advanced texts on homebrewing. Excellent discussions of mashing, including photos of several home setups involving coolers and plastic buckets, are presented in Charlie Papazian's *Complete Joy of Home Brewing*.

RIMS

To handle the large quantities of grain and water involved, brewers who mash often use dedicated multi-kettle systems with propane burners, which allow them to carefully control temperatures and handle large quantities of liquid easily. Some setups have built-in temperature gauges, as well as pumps and piping designed to recirculate the wort through the grain bed before it is released to the brewing kettle. These setups are sometimes called recirculating infusion mash systems (RIMS). Instructions for making them can be found on the Internet.

One commercially made RIMS system, Sabco Industries' Brew-Magic IV, uses recycled beer kegs to hold the water, grains, and wort. Through a series of valves (red handles), water heated in the sparge kettle (upper right) is pumped into the top of the mash kettle (upper left). Wort can be recirculated from the mash kettle through the pump (black box on the far right) and back to the kettle again, or it can be drained into the boil ket-

tle (lower left) and then into a fermenter. Propane jets beneath each tank, regulated by the temperature gauges, maintain the correct temperatures for the process.

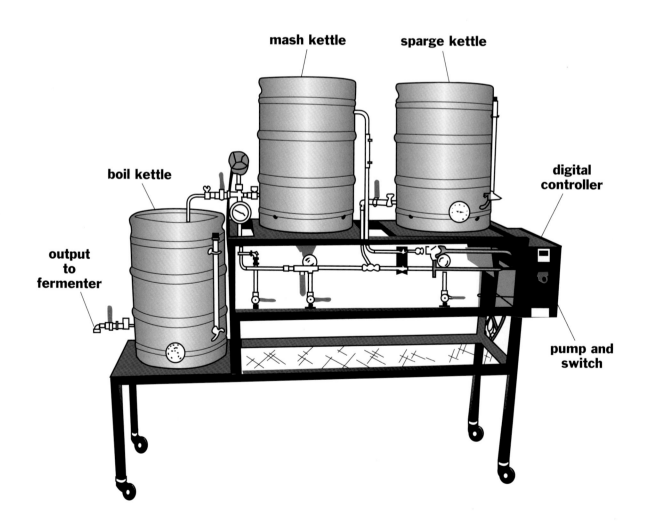

output to fermenter
boil kettle
mash kettle
sparge kettle
digital controller
pump and switch

Resources

Following are several sources of additional information for brewers.

ORGANIZATIONS

American Homebrewers Association
736 Pearl St.
Boulder, CO 80302
(303) 447-0816
(888) 822-6273 (U.S. and Canada only)
www.beertown.org
The largest national-level organization for American homebrewers and small craft brewers.

Other state and local organizations also exist.

LITERATURE

Papazian, Charlie. *Complete Joy of Home Brewing*, 3rd ed. New York: HarperResource, 2003.

Zymurgy, the journal of the American Homebrewers Association
   www.beertown.org/homebrewing/zymurgy.html
Brew Your Own
   5053 Main St., Suite A
   Manchester Center, VT 05255
   802-362-3981
   fax: 802-362-2377
   email: byo@byo.com
   www.byo.com
   How-to homebrew beer magazine. Good interactive website features recipes, columns, and a free first issue offer.
All about Beer
   501-H Washington St.
   Durham, NC 27701
   800-977-2337
   fax: 919-530-8160
   email: editor@allaboutbeer.com
   www.allaboutbeer.com/aabmhome.html
   Magazine published out of North Carolina. Information and several features available online.

WEBSITES

www.hbd.org The popular Homebrew Digest features ongoing discussions about various topics and a subscription-based email listserv.

www.realbeer.com Features active, moderated bulletin boards. Good events calendar at *www.realbeer.com/search/eventscalendar/index.php*

http://brewery.org/brewery/ A comprehensive, high-quality collection of information about the art and science of brewing beer.

www.beerinfo.com/siteidx.html This website is maintained by John Lock, the current editor of the Usenet newsgroup rec.food.drink.beer: *www.beerinfo.com/rfdb/faq.html*. The site index features a vast collection of links to brewing resources of all kinds. Good listing of primary source equipment and ingredients manufacturers at *www.beerinfo.com/brewstr/supplies.html*.

www.brewingtechniques.com Website for out-of-print brewing magazine from the 1990s. Contains a wealth of online articles and information, most accessible from *www.brewingtechniques.com/library/articleindex.html*.

www.howtobrew.com Comprehensive chapter-by-chapter brewing guide, written by John Palmer. Interesting appendixes cover metallurgy and building wort chillers and mashing tuns.

LEADING RETAILERS

Beer, Beer, and More Beer
This California-based supplier has a comprehensive selection of brewing equipment and supplies, as well as winemaking and coffee roasting equipment. Free shipping on orders over $49 Toll-free order number: 800-600-0033. Website: www.morebeer.com.
Southern California Retail Store
1506 Columbia Ave., Suite 12
Riverside, CA 92507
951-779-9971
Northern California Retail Store
995 Detroit Ave., Unit G
Concord, CA 94518
925-939-BEER (2337)

Midwest Homebrewing and Winemaking Supplies
Reputable supplier with high-quality starter kits for brewers.
5701 W. 36th Street
Minneapolis, MN 55416
952-925-9835
888-449-2739
www.midwestsupplies.com/

William's Brewing
Informative, beautifully illustrated free catalog available by request. Features dozens of beginners' kits in all beer styles, as well as winemaking and coffee-roasting supplies.
2594 Nicholson St.
San Leandro, CA 94577
order line: 800-759-6025
www.williamsbrewing.com/

St. Patrick's of Texas
Longtime brewing supply company. Now moving more toward large-scale equipment and supplies for commercial brewers, but some interesting advanced equipment for homebrewers is available.
1828 Fleischer Drive
Austin, TX 78728
512-989-9727
email: stpats@bga.com
www.stpats.com/

Grape and Granary
This well-known Ohio retailer has been in the business for ten years.
915 Home Ave.
Akron, OH 44310
800-695-9870
fax: 330-633-6794
www.grapeandgranary.com

Homebrew Heaven
Comprehensive selection. Catalog available via download online or by request.
9109 Evergreen Way
Everett, WA 98204
toll-free order line: 800-850-2739
fax: 425-290-8336
local: 425-355-8865
email: brewheaven@aol.com
www.homebrewheaven.com

Sabco Industries, Inc.
4511 South Avenue
Toledo, OH 43615
419-531-5347
fax: 419-531-7765
www.kegs.com

Stackpole Basics

All the Skills and Tools You Need to Get Started

- **Straightforward, expert instruction on a variety of crafts, hobbies, and sports**
- **Step-by-step, easy-to-follow format**
- **Current information on equipment and prices for the beginner**
- **Full-color photography and illustrations**
- **Convenient lay-flat spiral binding**

BASIC KNITTING
$19.95, 108 pages, 377 color photos,
50 color illustrations, 0-8117-3178-2

BASIC CANDLE MAKING
$19.95, 104 pages, 600 color photos,
0-8117-2476-X

BASIC STAINED GLASS MAKING
$19.95, 144 pages, 754 color photos,
24 illustrations, 0-8117-2846-3

BASIC DRIED FLOWER ARRANGING
$16.95, 96 pages, 234 color photos,
0-8117-2863-3

BASIC WOODWORKING
$19.95, 80 pages, 303 color photos,
0-8117-3113-8

BASIC PICTURE FRAMING
$19.95, 108 pages, 374 color photos,
0-8117-3109-X

BASIC JEWELRY MAKING
$19.95, 116 pages, 490 color photos,
12 illustrations, 0-8117-3263-0

BASIC HOMEBREWING
$19.95, 80 pages, 191 color photos,
0-8117-3259-2

Available at your favorite retailer,
or from Stackpole Books at (800) 732-3669

STACKPOLE BOOKS

www.stackpolebooks.com